WHAT
DO I DO
WITH A
MUSTARD
SEED?

WHAT DO I DO WITH A MUSTARD SEED?

by Phillip Eichman

Gospel Advocate Company
Nashville, Tennessee

Chapters 10, 11 and 12 contain exerpts from *The God of All Comfort: Hope for Christians in a World of Suffering* by Phillip Eichman (© 2002 by Phillip Eichman). Used by permission.

All scripture quotations, unless otherwise noted, are taken from the HOLY BIBLE: NEW KING JAMES VERSION. Copyright © 1988 Thomas Nelson, Inc. Used by permission. All rights reserved.

Published by Gospel Advocate Co.
1006 Elm Hill Pike, Nashville, TN 37210
http://www.gospeladvocate.com

ISBN-10: 0-89225-566-8
ISBN-13: 978-0-89225-566-5

Dedication

To those who walk each day by faith, knowing that
something better is waiting for them.

Acknowledgements

Special thanks to Judy Van Dyke for sharing her
knowledge of teenagers and helping this book become
a mustard seed of faith in their lives.

Table of Contents

Introduction

The expression "small as a mustard seed" must have been commonly used in Bible times. It comes from a mustard plant, actually an herb, which was grown for centuries in the region of the Mediterranean Sea. Parts of the plant were used in the making of medicines. It was also known for its tiny seed, much smaller than others, such as wheat or barley, for example, that were known at the time.

Jesus used this tiny seed more than once to illustrate something that He was teaching. On one occasion he used it to make a point regarding faith. In Matthew 17:20 Jesus said, "[I]f you have faith as a mustard seed, you will say to this mountain, 'Move from here to there,' and it will move; and nothing will be impossible for you." Jesus seems to be saying here that even a small amount of faith can do great things – something that is encouraging to me as I try to develop my own personal faith.

Another time Jesus told a parable using a mustard seed as an illustration. In Luke 13:18-19 we read: "Then He said, 'What is the kingdom of God like? And to what shall I compare it? It is like a mustard seed, which a man took and put in his garden; and it grew and became a large tree, and the birds of the air nested in its branches.' "

Again Jesus was talking about smallness. Like the tiny seed that grows into a large plant, things in God's kingdom may begin small but grow and develop into something much larger.

This again is encouraging when we realize that faith can grow and develop. If the faith that I have today is the same as the faith that I will have a year from now, then something is wrong. It would be like a plant that had failed to grow and mature.

As a young person studying this book, your faith is also young, but it can grow and develop as you mature in your knowledge and understanding of God and His Word.

The aim of this book is to help your faith grow. The topics were chosen for this very reason. The titles for the lessons are given as questions, and these are serious questions of life that each of us asks and must answer for ourselves. As you go through this study, it is my hope that you will begin to ask and answer these questions for yourself and in doing so your faith will grow like a mustard seed.

About This Book

Each chapter of this book contains a "Mustard Seed Moment" at the beginning to introduce the subject to be studied. It contains questions to consider as you read the chapter.

Each chapter ends with "Faith Builders," questions to review the chapter and its conclusions, as well as "Mountain Movers" – discussion starters and further life applications for the chapter's topic.

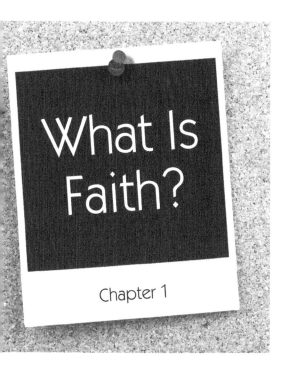

What Is Faith?

Chapter 1

"So Jesus said to them, ' ... for assuredly, I say to you, if you have faith as a mustard seed, you will say to this mountain, "Move from here to there," and it will move; and nothing will be impossible for you' " (Matthew 17:20).

Mustard Seed Moment

How do we determine the strength of our faith? Have we moved any mountains lately? What about the seemingly immovable mountains in our lives? What about hard-to-face problems? What about difficult choices or bad habits that we have fallen into that are hard to escape? What about family problems that seem like they will never improve?

If someone handed me a raw potato and a plastic drinking straw and challenged me to put the straw through the potato, would that be possible? Think how flimsy a plastic straw is compared to a potato. When the straw hits the potato, won't it bend? That's a logical assumption, but actually putting a straw through a potato is possible. You just have to know the trick. Here's how: hold the potato in the palm of your hand at about waist level. Then place the thumb of your other hand over the top end of the straw. Now, aim straight for the potato. With a quick thrust and keeping your thumb over the end of the straw, you should be able to put the straw through the potato. It should go completely through. The secret is holding your thumb over the end of the straw. It changes the air pressure in the straw and gives it the strength to puncture the potato. Sound impossible? With the help of one who knows the secret, it's possible!

What do I do with a mustard seed? How can we make our faith grow so the impossible is possible? How strong is our faith? Do we really believe that God can help us move the "mountains" in our lives – no matter how impossible the task might seem? We must strengthen our faith every day – through prayer and our actions. Things don't happen overnight, but our faith must remain strong in God and His love for us. In this chapter, we'll learn what the Bible teaches us about faith and how our faith can help us grow into what God wants us to be.

How Strong Is Your Faith?

The early Christians were often persecuted for their faith in Jesus. We can find examples of this persecution in the Bible itself, specifically in the book of Acts, as well as in historical documentation outside of the Bible. Many of us have heard, for example, of the Christians in the city of Rome who were forced to meet for worship in underground tombs, called catacombs, to avoid persecution.

Down through the centuries the persecution of people because of their religious beliefs has continued. Even today in some parts of the world, people are punished, imprisoned and even die because of their faith.

Is my faith that strong? Would I have enough faith to die for something or someone? How can I develop this kind of faith? I don't know about you, but when I read or think about religious persecution, I begin to ask questions such as these about my own faith.

"Faith" is a word that is sometimes misunderstood or misused in everyday language. In this chapter we will look at the question, "What is faith?" In doing so, we will try to develop a definition of the word and define how it is used in relation to God and the Bible.

The Meaning of the Word "Faith"

Originally, the Bible was written in Hebrew and Greek and translated into the English versions with which we are familiar. In both the Old Testament and New Testament, several words are translated as "faith," "faithful," "believe" or "belief." (See Genesis 15:6; Exodus 4:5; John 1:7; and Romans 3:22-24.)

The meanings of the original words for "faith," however, go beyond a mental acceptance of something. These words can also mean "trustworthiness," "dependability" or "confidence" and are often translated to reflect this meaning. (See Psalm 33:4; Proverbs 13:17; Hosea 5:9; Philippians 2:24; and 2 Timothy 2:2.)

Thus, we can see that "faith" as identified in the Bible is more than simple belief. The original words also suggest trust, dependability, assurance and confidence in what is believed.

A Definition or Description of "Faith"

The Bible itself gives a definition for "faith." This description is found in Hebrews, a letter of encouragement written to Christians struggling with their own faith. In Hebrews 11:1 the writer begins an entire chapter about the subject of faith with these words: "Now faith is being *sure* of what we hope for and *certain* of what we do not see" (NIV).

We have already noted that the words used for "faith" in both the Old Testament and New Testament carry with them the idea of confidence, assurance and trust. In this passage the author of Hebrews used additional terms that further emphasize this aspect of faith.

In the first part of the verse, the author indicates that faith is "being sure of what we hope for." The word translated as "sure" (or "assurance" in the Revised Standard Version and New American Standard Bible) originally meant something that provides support or structure, such as the foundation of a building. In addition, the author describes "faith" as that which makes us "certain of what we do not see" (translated as "evidence" in the New King James Version, King James Version, and the New Living Translation). This phrase was originally one that referred to providing or establishing evidence, as in a court of law.

The author also associates the word "hope" with "faith" in this verse. "Hope" is used in various ways in everyday language. Usually, the meaning would best be described as merely a wish or desire for something to happen. The word for "hope" used in the New Testament, however, meant much more than just wishful thinking; it also carried with it the idea of expectation and anticipation.

All these images – the idea of a sturdy foundation, the supporting evidence in a court of law, and the associated anticipation and expectation of hope – help us to understand further the meaning of "faith" as used in the Bible. In examining how the original words have been translated and the definition or description of "faith" in Hebrews 11:1, we see that the Bible writers had a very definite meaning in mind when they used the term "faith." For them, faith was much more than mere mental acceptance. Faith was something to trust, something to build one's life upon, something to hope for.

Faith as a Way of Looking at the World Around Us

Up to this point, we have seen that faith involves assurance, certainty and confidence. But faith is much more. It can give us a way of understanding the world around us.

Consider Hebrews 11:3: "By faith we understand that the worlds were framed by the word of God, so that the things which are seen were not made of things which are visible." This is a basic faith statement that God formed the universe out of nothing.

Someone may ask, "Hasn't science given us a better explanation than that old myth?" The answer is no. Science actually cannot answer questions related to the ultimate origin of the universe. Science can go back only so far – to the beginning. This verse, however, transcends the beginning and takes us back beyond time itself.

The very best scientific explanations cannot explain how matter, the stuff that the universe is made of, came into being. Scientists believe that matter has always existed or was made in some way that science hasn't discovered yet. As Christians we accept by faith that God created the universe. Whether a person chooses faith in God or faith in some unknown process, that choice is a matter of faith.

Hebrews 11:3 expresses a basic belief that serves as the foundation of how Christians look at the world. It takes us beyond the beginning of time. It offers a first step in understanding the world around us and helps us make sense of our relationship with the physical world and with God, the Creator. This verse also represents the beginning point for our faith because it ties together the physical universe that we *can* see and our faith in God, whom we *cannot* see.

What About Doubts?

Although reluctant to admit that we have doubts, many of us do have questions and uncertainties about our faith at times. When we are troubled by doubts, it is helpful first to remember that doubt is not the same as unbelief. A person with faith may still have questions regarding that faith. Unbelief, however, is an absence of faith and a conscious choice. A person must make a decision not to believe.

Doubts can certainly lead to unbelief, but they can also lead to a stronger, growing faith. It all depends on what a person does with his or her doubts. A faith that has not been tested is seldom a strong, viable faith. Doubts and uncertainties regarding faith can provide a time of testing and spiritual growth that leads to a stronger faith.

In his 2004 book, *Beyond Words: Daily Readings in the ABC's of Faith*, American author Frederick Buechner calls doubts the "ants in the pants of faith." Just as "ants in the pants" lead one to action, so should doubts lead to study, reflection and spiritual growth.

Editor and author Philip Yancey has suggested that we should question our doubts. Why is it that when problems arise, we tend to question our faith? Why not question our doubts as well? In doing so, doubts often can have positive rather than negative effects on our faith and can be a source of growth rather than discouragement.

When confronting doubts, we should remember the important point that faith by its very nature requires some degree of uncertainty. If this were not the case, then faith would not be faith at all. As Paul wrote to the Christians living in Corinth, "For we walk by faith, not by sight" (2 Corinthians 5:7). If we could see or know everything, then faith would not be necessary. All faith involves that little bit of uncertainty that requires us to make a decision. That does not mean, however, that our Christian faith must be "blind" because God has provided a basis for our faith by revealing Himself to us in His creation and through His Word.

Faith Builders

1. What is the basic meaning of "faith" as used in the Bible?

2. Does the way in which people today use the word "faith" really reflect the meaning of the word?

3. How would you define "faith" in your own words? Is this the same definition you would have given before this study?

4. What does Hebrews 11:1 tell us about faith?

5. What does Hebrews 11:3 tell us about the universe? How does this fact relate to our faith?

6. Can a person have doubts and still believe? What are some good ways to handle our doubts?

Mountain Movers

In this chapter, we learned that faith "by its very nature requires some degree of uncertainty. If this were not the case, then faith would not be faith at all."

- What does the above statement mean?
- What are some elements of our faith we might be unsure about?
- What are some things about our faith we may not understand?
- Is it okay to question why God allows certain things to happen?
- Does it show a lack of faith if we question God?
- Can you think of a specific situation that caused you or someone you know to question God? What was the result?
- What are some practical ways we can strengthen our faith?

Sometimes there are no good answers for life's questions. Sometimes we find the answers we need in God's Word – or at least some comfort and hope. Romans 15:4 states, "For whatever things were written before were written for our learning, that we through the patience and comfort of the Scriptures might have hope." Sometimes answers aren't easy or there are no answers at all. In those times, we just have to have faith that God will carry us through. Sometimes that's our answer.

Do you believe God can make the impossible possible? Just as it seemed impossible to put a plastic straw through a potato in this chapter's "Mustard Seed Moment," God knows how to make the impossible possible. He holds the secret in His wisdom and power. Our faith connects us to that power.

We learned in this chapter that doubting or questioning our faith is not the same as unbelief. "Unbelief is an absence of faith and a conscious choice. A person must make a decision not to believe."

- Have you ever met an atheist, a person who does not believe in God?
- Have you ever met someone who says he or she believes in God but doesn't show it in their actions?
- How do you truly show that you believe in God?
- Have you ever been disappointed in a friend who said one thing but did another?
- How important is our example?

Share some experiences with the class. Discuss ways we can be firmer in our faith when having to deal with tough situations and difficult people.

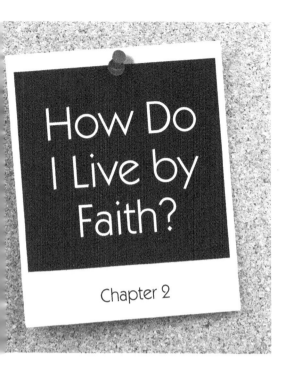

How Do
I Live by
Faith?

Chapter 2

"For we know that if our earthly house, this tent, is destroyed, we have a building from God, a house not made with hands ... . So we are always confident, knowing that while we are at home in the body we are absent from the Lord. For we walk by faith, not by sight" (2 Corinthians 5:1, 6-7).

Mustard Seed Moment

Let's suppose I want some beautiful flowers. I don't want to just go buy them, so I find a flower pot, fill it with rich soil and plant flower seeds down in the soil. I know that water helps flowers to grow, so I pour a little bit of water into the flower pot every day.

Let's suppose I also want some cookies. Instead of purchasing a package of cookies at the grocery store, I decide to grow my own cookies. I find a flower pot and fill it with rich soil. Then I crumble up some cookies and plant the crumbs in the soil. I know that milk goes well with cookies, so surely some milk would help my cookies grow. Every day I pour a little bit of milk into the flower pot.

Which of my plantings would sprout first? Of course, the flowers would sprout, and the cookies would not. If I take care of my flower plant, keep it watered, and give it the right amount of sunshine and care, it will probably grow into beautiful flowers one day.

Why can't I grow cookies from cookie crumbs and milk in a flower pot? That is ridiculous, right? Why? It's because I know how cookies are made. I already know cookies do not grow in a flower pot. I know that cookies come from someone mixing a batter and baking them. I have knowledge that I can purchase cookies from the grocery store or make them myself.

I have faith that a flower will grow from a seed. That faith is based on my knowledge and experience in planting. The reason I would spend the time to plant the flower seeds is that I have faith there will be a result from my efforts. My faith is based on my previous knowledge and experience; I believe something is true (the flower will grow) although I can't see the results yet.

How do we gain knowledge to successfully grow our faith in God? He gave us a definition of faith in Hebrews 11:1: "Now faith is the substance [realization] of things hoped for, the evidence [confidence] of things not seen." The Bible gives us the knowledge we need to know how to grow our faith. Although it's something we can't see right now, we believe planting seeds in the soil will produce flowers one day. We have faith that it will happen. In the same way, our knowledge of the Bible and God's promises gives us the faith that we can live in heaven with Him one day. How can we nurture our seeds of faith and help them grow? Bible study, worship, prayer and encouragement from other Christians.

What do I do with a mustard seed? In this chapter, we'll learn more of how to plant those seeds of faith in our hearts and in our lives so that we can grow to be the Christians God wants us to be. We should have faith that God will grow great things in our lives if we plant the right seeds and nurture them properly. We can have faith that there will be a result from our efforts – God has promised us an eternal home in heaven one day. In the previous chapter we looked at the meaning of faith. In this chapter we will investigate what it means to live our lives by faith.

Choosing a Life of Faith

When it is time for you to make a major purchase, how do you make the decision? Some people see something they like and simply buy it on the spot. For others it is a long process of weeks or even months. They read reports, compare options, look at prices, and surf the Internet for more information. Finally, at the end of this lengthy process of comparing, evaluating and weighing information, they make the purchase. For those individuals it is an important decision that requires careful study and evaluation.

Faith is like that, too. Choosing a life of faith should not be based on impulse but rather a careful decision should be based on evaluation and weighing of evidence. Only then can a person have the fullest confidence in what he or she believes.

What Faith Is Not

Many people have misconceptions about faith, particularly during their early years as a Christian when their personal faith is developing. And although it's important to learn what faith is, it's just as important to learn what faith is *not*. As we take a look at some common misconceptions about faith, ask yourself if they sound familiar to you.

• **Faith is not merely blind acceptance.** It is certainly true that faith can cause someone to accept something unquestioningly. It is also true that the Bible tells us, "For we walk by faith, not by sight" (2 Corinthians 5:7). This verse, however, does not demand that our faith be blind. In fact, the Bible teaches that we can have evidence upon which to base our faith. Several passages teach that we can see evidence of God in the physical world. Psalm 19:1, for example, refers to evidence of God's creative work in the universe. Romans 1:18-23 is another example. In fact, Paul is quite emphatic when he states that there is no excuse for not seeing God in the things that He has made.

We also have evidence for basing our faith in God on the Bible itself. This will be the subject of the next two chapters.

• **Faith is not the last resort.** For some people faith is a last resort when nothing else will work. You may have heard someone say, "Well, I guess we will just have to take that by faith." This, however, is an attitude of defeat and contrary to faith as described in the Bible. Actually, faith is the first step in a relationship with God (Hebrews 11:6) and the basis for living the Christian life. Faith is the first thing we should look to, not the last.

• **Faith is not something to embrace only when life becomes difficult.** When things are going well, many people tend to ignore faith and think about it only during times of illness or other problems in life. Faith certainly can be a source of strength in such times, but it is seen in quite a different manner in Scripture. It is the basis for an ongoing relationship with God and a foundation of the Christian life in both good times and bad.

• **Faith is not surrender.** Some people may believe it necessary to surrender or give up in order to have faith. For them, faith is essentially seen as defeat. This is especially true in our society where self-reliance and self-sufficiency are highly valued.

Faith in God may require a person to give up certain things. The individual, however, does not just grudgingly forfeit these things. Instead he gives them up freely. Doing so is a conscious decision, not the result of defeat or failure.

What Faith Is

• **Faith is a decision.** Faith results from a decision a person makes. In Hebrews 11 we read about several people of faith from the Old Testament. These were not weak individuals. They were intelligent, capable people of faith. Each made a decision and then followed through with it. Among them are Abel, who made a sacrifice to God that was accepted although that of his brother Cain was not (v. 4); Noah, who was told to build an ark (v. 7); and Abraham, who was told to leave his home and move to another country (vv. 8-10).

When we read these examples, we can see how faith was an integral part of the lives of these Old Testament characters. Their lives were lives of faith, and that is why they have been remembered. In each case they made a decision based upon faith and then followed through with that decision.

• **Faith is something we use every day.** All of us have some kind of faith whether we admit it or not. Faith is, in fact, something we use every day. We may call it belief, trust, acceptance or something more technical like an assumption or a presupposition – but it is still faith, just called by another name.

Consider these examples. Faith and science may seem to be incompatible, but faith is actually an integral part of any scientific investigation. All of science is based on assumptions or presuppositions. A scientist assumes (or has faith) that his senses can be trusted and that his instruments are accurate. A scientist further assumes (or has faith) that he or she can use reasoning to draw conclusions and form hypotheses.

Driving a car requires a great deal of faith. When you drive a car, you assume (or have faith) that the wheels will remain attached, the brakes will work, and the car will steer in the direction in which you turn the wheel. Cars traveling on a two-lane road at 55 miles per hour pass each other within a few feet. Each driver assumes (or has faith) that the other driver will remain on his side of the road.

Faith is definitely a part of everyday life. We may not recognize it as faith – we may call it by another name – but faith is still very important to each one of us.

• **Faith and proof.** Someone may say, "You cannot prove without a doubt that God exists or that the Bible is His Word." This statement is certainly correct. It is impossible to prove with absolute certainty that God exists or that the Bible really is His Word. Actually, proving *anything* with absolute certainty is quite difficult.

Part of the problem is that the words "prove" and "proof" often are used incorrectly. The term "scientifically proven," for example, does not imply absolute certainty. A scientist will form a hypothesis, examine the evidence and draw a conclusion. That conclusion will be based on assumptions that he or she has already made. One of those assumptions will be exactly how certain he needs to be to accept the hypothesis. Seldom, if ever, is the level of certainty set for 100 percent. Even with a "scientific proof," some degree of uncertainty generally remains.

Faith in God, Jesus or the Bible is very similar. A person must examine the evidence and draw a conclusion based on certain assumptions. It isn't possible to "prove" that God exists or that the Bible is His Word with 100 percent certainty, but faith can be based on evidence in a manner similar to a scientific proof.

• **Faith is reasonable.** Often people see faith as something illogical, unreasonable and irrational. Many people view faith as something held only by uneducated and superstitious people. This view may be true in some cases – people often believe in some very strange things.

But faith, in a biblical sense, can be logical, reasonable and rational. As we have seen, faith results from a conscious decision based on evidence. We can look at the evidence of God in the natural world and in the Bible. We can also see how God has affected the lives of Christians. Based on the evidence, we can make a decision to believe.

Nowhere in the Bible do we read that we are expected to make a decision without some type of evidence. The Bible makes claims that can be tested and proved to be either true or false. The Bible makes reference, for example, to historical people, places and events that can be checked and verified or rejected.

Christians are, in fact, expected to have a reasonable faith. In 1 Peter 3:15 we read, "Always be ready to give a defense to everyone who asks you a reason for the hope that is in you, with meekness and fear." Some versions of the Bible translate "make a defense" as "give an answer." The original word for this phrase referred to a legal case and the supplying of evidence to support that case. A lawyer "defends" his client by supplying evidence to support his client's innocence. In a similar manner we should be able to supply evidence for why we believe what we believe.

Faith Builders

1. What are some common misconceptions of faith?

2. How is faith actually a decision?

3. What are some examples of faith in everyday life?

4. What are some other words that might be used in place of "faith"?

5. What does "proving" or "proof" have to do with faith?

Mountain Movers

If we had to prove that God was real in a court of law, what evidence would we have? Could we prove beyond the shadow of a doubt that God exists and that He made everything? Pretend we are in a courtroom. Let some members of the class pretend to be defendants. They believe there is no God and that faith in God is ridiculous. Let other members of the class act as the prosecution. Their job is to prove why the defendants are wrong.

We need to realize that proving God exists beyond the shadow of a doubt is impossible. That is where our faith kicks in. A person either believes the Bible or he doesn't. A person either believes in a God that created the universe or he doesn't. However, we should be able to show evidence for why we believe what we believe. We can share our faith and our logic and what the Bible teaches with someone else, but that person may or may not accept it. Ultimately, we can go to the Bible and give evidence and go to science, history and fossil records to prove the Bible is true in its creation story, but there will always be questions from believers and unbelievers alike.

As we learned in Chapter 1, unbelief in God is a conscious choice. The courtroom scenario should have been a profitable exercise in helping us examine why we believe in God and why others may choose not to believe.

- Were both sides (the defense and the prosecution) able to make valid points?
- What feelings were stirred up during the debate? Frustration? Uncertainty? Agreeing to disagree?

Faith requires some degree of uncertainty. We can't explain everything. The Bible explains enough for us to believe – but it doesn't explain everything. That is a fact. Being honest with others about that fact is important. But remember, if we knew everything and knew all the answers, then our faith would not be faith at all!

- How would you explain to another person that God gave us enough information in the Bible? How much is enough?
- What if a person asked you a question for which the Bible does not have an answer?
- Is it enough for a person to just believe what he or she wants to believe? Why?

Remember, faith is a personal commitment. Our faith in God should be what matters most in our lives. God wants our faith to grow, and His Word shows us how.

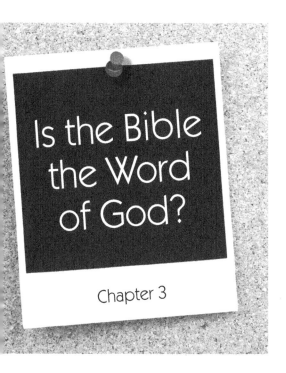

Is the Bible
the Word
of God?

Chapter 3

"But He said, 'More
than that, blessed
are those who
hear the word of
God and keep it!' "
(Luke 11:28).

Mustard Seed Moment

I would imagine most of us have good cooks in our families. Let's say that one of our grandmothers makes the best lasagna ever. She doesn't find it in the frozen-foods section at the supermarket; her lasagna is home-made. We ask Grandma for her lasagna recipe, and she gladly shares it with us. One of us decides to try to make lasagna just like Grandma. He's not a great cook, but he believes he can do it because he has Grandma's personal recipe, and he has the right ingredients. He has trusted his grand-mother to give him all the right instructions. So to make the lasagna suc-cessfully, he must have faith in her recipe and follow exactly what the recipe tells him to do.

What do I do with a mustard seed? The Bible is our recipe for life. God's recipe for how to live our lives faithfully can be trusted because God inspired the men who wrote it. We can have faith that what we believe is true because we love and trust God. In this chapter, we will determine reasons why we should follow God's recipe, the instructions found in His Word.

Is the Bible Really Different?

The Bible is one of the best-known books of all history and a very special book. It contains the words of God. Some people, however, think of the Bible simply as one book among many and no more special than any other great book. Is the Bible really different from other books? Is it really the very words of God Himself?

Such questions are crucial in considering the information contained in the Bible. If the Bible is merely the work of some human writers, then we need not be very concerned about its contents. It would be little more than any other book of moral stories. If, on the other hand, the Bible is unique and is the Word of God, then we can have confidence in the Bible and its claims.

We often hear that the Bible is the "inspired Word of God." What is inspiration, and what does it mean to be inspired? Often the Bible is also called God's "revelation" or His "revealed will." What do these terms mean? We will look briefly at the meanings of "inspiration" and "revelation" and examine how they relate to an understanding of the Bible as the Word of God.

The Meaning of "Inspiration"

"Inspiration" and "inspired" are words often used in reference to the Bible. What does it mean to say that the Bible is inspired or that we have received the Bible through the process of inspiration? The original word literally means "God-breathed" and is found only once in the Bible (2 Timothy 3:16-17). This word has been translated into English as "inspiration of God" (New King James Version and King James Version) or "inspired by God" (New American Standard Bible and New Living Translation). Other versions translate the word as "God-breathed" (New International Version) or simply "given by God" (New Century Version).

Although 2 Timothy 3:16-17 is the only place where the word translated as "inspiration" is used, the writers of the Bible agree that they were indeed speaking for God. In the Old Testament alone, more than 2,400 references attribute the message to God (see the Appendix for examples). The prophets especially were noted for such attribution – and rightly so: the word "prophet" means "one who speaks for God." The prophets were literally God's spokesmen who communicated His will to others.

The writers of the New Testament recognized that the Old Testament was from God and used it as the basis for much of their teaching

(Matthew 1:22-23; Acts 4:24-26). The New Testament writers also recognized that they were speaking for God (2 Peter 1:19-21).

Jesus taught the apostles that they would be guided by the Holy Spirit (John 14:26; 16:13). Through this guidance by the Holy Spirit, these men established the church, served as its first leaders, and wrote much of the New Testament.

How Were the Writers Inspired?

How did the writers of the Bible receive these words from God? Some people believe the authors were some kind of secretary to whom God "dictated" every word. The style, vocabulary and other literary features, however, differ from one writer to another. For this reason it seems God guided the writers in terms of content but allowed them some freedom of expression in their writing.

The Bible actually does not explain how the authors were inspired. The reference in 2 Timothy 3:16-17 merely tells us that "all Scripture is given by inspiration of God." A related verse in 2 Peter 1:21 indicates that "holy men of God spoke as they were moved by the Holy Spirit." However, these verses tell us little about how inspiration occurred. The Bible clearly claims to have come from God. How this was accomplished, however, is not fully explained.

What Is "Revelation"?

The Greek word translated as "revelation" is found numerous times in the New Testament and literally means "to uncover or unveil." Thus, revelation is the process that allows a person to understand something previously hidden or unknown. Revelation is the process of divine communication of knowledge that could not be obtained in any other manner – or, stated more simply, revelation is the process by which God makes His will known to human beings.

The actual details of how the writers of the Bible received this revelation are not given. A few verses, however, refer to individuals who received a revelation from God (Galatians 1:11-12; 2 Peter 1:21; Revelation 1:1-2) – revelation that was evidently a supernatural or miraculous process involving the Holy Spirit.

Unlike inspiration, which God ceased to use when the writing of His

Word was completed, revelation is still at work today. That does not mean to say, however, that God still reveals information in a miraculous manner to individuals today as He did in the case of the apostles; that aspect of revelation is no longer taking place. God, however, does reveal Himself to us through the Bible and in His creation.

Types of Revelation

Basically, two types of revelation are from God: general and specific. General revelation is what we can learn about God through His creation. References such as Romans 1:18-20 indicate that we can see evidence of God's existence, His intelligence and His creative power in the physical universe He has made. This form of revelation, however, is limited to general information about God. We cannot, for example, learn about God's love and grace, or how we are to worship, obey or serve God through general revelation. This information comes only through specific revelation.

God has made known, through specific revelation, things that we otherwise would be unable to know or understand. This specific information has been revealed in various ways. In the Old Testament, for example, God spoke directly to the patriarchs, gave the Law to Moses, and spoke through prophets and others as well. The New Testament, God's final revelation, also contains specific revelation. Within its pages we can read about the life of Jesus, details about the church, and about God's expectations of His people today.

Perhaps God's greatest revelation was His Son, Jesus, who came to earth in the form of a man (see John 1:1-5, 14). In the person of Jesus, we can know more about the nature of God than through all the other revelations. In Him we see God as one of us.

The Extent of Revelation

We close by examining some additional aspects of God's revelation:
• **Revelation is limited.** That is not to say that God is limited, but that He has limited the details of His revelation. Sometimes we would like to know more, but God evidently has not chosen to reveal everything we might want to know. The Bible, however, contains enough information for us to learn how to obey God, live in a right relationship

with Him in this life, and live with Him eternally in the next.

• **Revelation is progressive.** The Bible begins with general information and proceeds to more specific information. It begins with an account of the creation of the universe, the earth and human beings, and then moves on, expanding and developing more specific themes.

• **Revelation is final.** Although some may claim otherwise, God's revelation is final, completed with the final book of the New Testament. We are to receive no more miraculous revelations from God (1 Corinthians 13:9-10; Jude 3). God has completed the task of revealing His will to mankind. Everything we need to know is found in the Scriptures.

• **Revelation is sufficient.** Although we often would like to have more information, God has provided all we really need to know in order to live in a right relationship with Him and with others (2 Timothy 3:16-17).

Faith Builders

1. What claims are made in the Bible regarding its origin and contents? Is this important? If so, why?

2. What does the word "inspiration" mean when used in reference to the Bible? Is this any different from the "inspiration" of an artist or a writer?

3. What does the word "revelation" mean? How is this related to the contents of the Bible?

4. What are the two types of revelation? What are some examples of each one?

5. What is the significance of saying that God's revelation is final and sufficient?

Mountain Movers

Read 2 Timothy 3:16-17 again: "All Scripture is given by inspiration of God, and is profitable for doctrine, for reproof, for correction, for instruction in righteousness, that the man of God may be complete, thoroughly equipped for every good work." To fully understand these verses, define the words "doctrine," "reproof," "correction," "instruction," "complete" and "equipped" as used in these verses. Discuss how each definition proves the Bible is profitable for "every good work."

- How can God's Word strengthen our faith?
- What specific revelations in the Bible help strengthen your faith the most?

What sets the Bible apart from other books? Are its teachings outdated? Does it have anything to say to us today? Consider this statement: "God gave us the Bible for a reason. Why did He give it to us if He didn't want us to read it, study it and live it?"

- Is it important to follow all the commands in the Bible? Why doesn't everyone believe that?
- Is one religion as good as another?

As you study the Bible more, your faith grows, your knowledge grows, and your ability to teach others grows. If you are serious about growing your faith, you must truly believe that the Bible is important in your life. And you can't just think it – you have to put your faith into action.

Just like the tiny mustard seed grows into a tree that shoots out large branches, your faith can grow and you can branch out and influence others. The potential is endless with God on your side! To help increase our faith, we need to commit ourselves to serious study of God's Word. That must be an important element in our lives, or our faith will not live up to its potential. Increase your faith. Know that God's Word is true, and pledge to be diligent in sharing His Word with others.

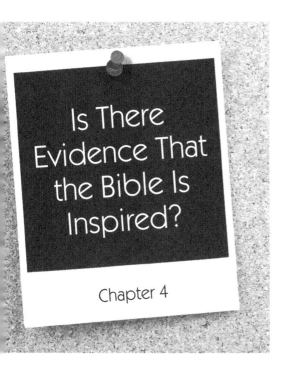

Is There Evidence That the Bible Is Inspired?

Chapter 4

"[F]or prophecy never came by the will of man, but holy men of God spoke as they were moved by the Holy Spirit" (2 Peter 1:21).

Mustard Seed Moment

What ingredients would be needed to make homemade chocolate chip cookies? We'd need some flour, baking soda, salt, butter, sugar, brown sugar, vanilla extract, eggs, chocolate chips and nuts. How would the ingredients taste if a person tried to eat them separately? Would she want to try a sip of vanilla extract or crack a raw egg into her mouth? Would she enjoy a spoonful of flour or baking soda? What about a big bite of butter? Of course, a few chocolate chips or nuts wouldn't taste bad; but the point is, it wouldn't make any sense for a person to eat the ingredients separately. The ingredients need to be combined to make a successful cookie dough. Each ingredient by itself is necessary, but to accomplish the finished product desired, the ingredients need to be mixed together and baked according to the directions.

The Bible is a perfect mixture of books. Each book by itself is very important, but to get the benefit of the whole "cookie," the books should be studied together. The 66 books of the Bible were written by approximately 40 different men. The writers came from different backgrounds. Some were tentmakers, shepherds, kings, fishermen, prophets – even a doctor. These men separately, through the inspiration of God by the Holy Spirit, wrote one united message. Only by God's inspiration could this complete and successful mixture have been accomplished (2 Peter 1:21).

What do I do with a mustard seed? Just as a person combines ingredients to make cookies, God was able to blend the inspired books together to create His Word. In this chapter, we will strengthen our faith in the inspiration of God's Word and its ability to fully equip us "for every good work" (2 Timothy 3:16-17).

Examining the Evidence

Antiques Roadshow has become a popular program on public television. The show travels from one city to another, and a panel of experts identifies and appraises antiques and collectibles brought in by the public. Often these items are determined to be rare and valuable. At other times, however, the item thought by its owner to be valuable turns out to be a fake.

Suppose, for example, someone brought in what appears to be a signed first edition of *The Adventures of Tom Sawyer*. How would the experts examine and appraise this book? They would look at the binding, the paper and the printing and compare them with other known first editions. They also would examine the signature, looking at the ink and comparing it with other signatures of the author. Only after careful examination would the experts agree that the book is, in fact, an authentic, signed first edition.

The same is true when we examine whether the Bible is genuine. It is not the only religious book in our world today. Like a panel of experts, we need to examine the Bible carefully in order to determine whether it is what it claims to be. If the Bible is the Word of God, then we should be able to see evidence that it is a very special book. Something about the Bible should set it apart from other such books. A careful study of the Bible will, in fact, reveal that evidence exists to support this conclusion.

The Claims of the Bible

As we learned in the last chapter, the Bible clearly and emphatically claims to be a God-breathed, or inspired, message. If this is so, then the Bible cannot be dismissed as a book of moral stories, for it claims to have come from a divine being. Numerous examples from both the Old Testament and New Testament can be cited to show that the message in the Bible indeed claims to be from God. Some of these are listed in the Appendix. You are encouraged to look up these references to see for yourself what the Bible says about its origins.

The Influence of the Bible

Skeptics have always been critical of the Bible and Christianity. However, a careful and unbiased study of history will reveal that the Bible has had a positive influence on mankind. Wherever the Bible has been used as a guide, civilization has been raised to a higher level. This is because the Bible emphasizes positive traits such as honesty, respect for others, compassion and kindness.

Certainly, down through history some individuals, including world leaders, have intentionally misused teachings from the Bible to advance their own selfish causes. These people, however, are the exceptions. In fact, many problems that have occurred during the course of world history can be traced back to a failure to follow the Bible's teachings.

The Unusual Style of the Bible

The style of the Bible is unique in literature. One of the first things a reader will notice is its brevity. The writers dealt with crucial issues in a brief, concise manner. Some examples include:

1. the origin of the universe, earth, living things and humans (Genesis 1–2);
2. Jesus' baptism (Matthew 3:13-17);
3. the Transfiguration (Matthew 17:1-8);
4. the execution of James, the first apostle to die (Acts 12:2); and
5. the burial of Stephen, the first Christian to die for his faith (Acts 8:2).

Another unusual aspect of the Bible involves the impartiality of its writers. Important characters in the Bible are sometimes described in a very frank, impartial and, at times, embarrassing manner:

1. Noah planted a vineyard and became drunk with the wine (Genesis 9:20-23).

2. Abraham lied about his wife, Sarah (Genesis 12:10-20; 20:1-18).
3. David committed adultery with Bathsheba (2 Samuel 11:1-27).
4. Peter denied Jesus (Matthew 26:69-75).

The Unity of the Bible

The Bible is not one book, but rather a collection of books written during a period of about 1,600 years by as many as 40 different people. These authors were from different cultural and social backgrounds and used at least three different languages. Skeptics have tried for centuries to find mistakes and contradictions in the Bible. Certainly, the Bible contains some difficult passages, but no major mistakes or contradictions have been found. Even by itself, the unity of the Bible would be enough to demonstrate that such a book would be impossible without guidance from the Holy Spirit.

Scientific and Medical Accuracy of the Bible

The Bible is not a medical or scientific book. It is, however, accurate whenever medical or scientific subjects are discussed. In fact, the level of medical knowledge portrayed in the Old Testament is much greater than one might expect from a group of people such as the Israelites. We read about such medical or hygienic practices as:
1. food restrictions for the prevention of disease;
2. quarantine of diseased persons;
3. burial of wastes; and
4. washing after contact with disease.

(See Leviticus 11–15 for details about these practices.)

The Bible also contains some scientific information. The rules for basic hygiene mentioned above, for example, have been substantiated by modern scientific investigation. We can add to them two other interesting examples of basic science found in Scripture:
1. Both male and female are necessary in the reproductive process ("seed of the woman"), as read in Genesis 3:15.
2. Blood is necessary for life, as read in Leviticus 17:11.

The scientific basis for both of these examples was unknown at the time they were written. In fact, not until the 20th century were these ideas fully documented and accepted by scientists.

Historical Accuracy

We must remember that the Bible is not a history book. However, the geography, place names, people and historical events recorded in the Bible have been found to be correct and accurate. Many of these have been verified by discoveries made by archaeologists, particularly during the last two centuries. Just a few examples of these discoveries include:

1. The palace of Sargon, king of Assyria (as mentioned in Isaiah 20:1), was discovered in 1843 by Paul Botta.
2. Mesha, king of Moab (as mentioned in 2 Kings 3:4), is named in an inscription on what is called the Moabite or Mesha Stone, discovered in 1869.
3. A large hexagonal column of baked clay has been discovered that describes the exploits of Sennacherib, king of Assyria (as mentioned in 2 Kings 18–19 and 2 Chronicles 32), including the siege of Jerusalem. It also mentions King Hezekiah by name.
4. Shalmaneser, king of Assyria (as mentioned in 2 Kings 17:3-6), left a stone pillar describing his life that includes a carving of Jehu, king of Israel, paying tribute.
5. Cyrus, king of Persia (as mentioned in 2 Chronicles 36:22-23), issued a decree allowing captive people to return to their homes. A stone cylinder with an inscription of the decree is in the British Museum.

Prophecy and Fulfillment

Further evidence for the inspiration of the Bible comes from prophecies and their fulfillment. The following list contains several examples of prophecies and their fulfillment from the books of Amos and Micah; many also can be verified by nonreligious historical sources.

1. Damascus will be conquered (Amos 1:3-5). Tiglath-Pileser, king of Assyria, destroyed Damascus in 732 B.C.

2. Gaza, Ashdod and Ashkelon will be destroyed (Amos 1:6-8). These cities were destroyed over a period of time by several different armies.
3. Tyre will be destroyed by fire (Amos 1:9-10). Sargon II, king of Assyria, destroyed Tyre in 722 B.C.
4. Moab will be burned and the judge removed (Amos 2:1-3). Nebuchadnezzar, king of Babylon, destroyed Moab in 582 B.C.
5. Jerusalem will be destroyed (Amos 2:4-5). Nebuchadnezzar, king of Babylon, attacked Jerusalem and burned the city in 586 B.C.
6. Samaria will be destroyed (Amos 3:12-15; Micah 1:6). Sargon II, king of Assyria, captured Samaria in 722 B.C.

Other Facts About the Bible

The circulation of the Bible throughout history exceeds that of any other book, and it is the most published book in the world. The Bible is also the most translated book in history. It was the first significant book to be translated into another language (the Septuagint, a Greek translation of the Hebrew Old Testament), and it has been translated into more languages than any other book in history.

The survival of the Bible through time is also unique for any written document. More early manuscripts exist of the New Testament, for example, than any other ancient book. And those manuscripts are dated much closer to the time of their original writing than the manuscripts of any other ancient book.

The Bible is probably the most carefully examined, analyzed and studied book in history. The text of the original languages has been studied carefully to ensure that we have the most accurate text possible. Most of the English translations we use today also have been painstakingly checked and rechecked many times for accuracy in translation from the original languages.

Finally, as pure literature, the Bible is unique, clearly standing apart from all other works of literature. Examples of these unique features include the following:

1. The Bible contains material that is unsurpassed in literature, such as the creation account, the Psalms, the Beatitudes and the parables.
2. The scope of the Bible begins with the creation of the universe and moves through the history of Israel, Jesus' life and the beginning of the church, and ends with the final events of human history.
3. The Bible deals with subjects important to our existence, such as life, death and marital and family relationships.
4. The Bible emphasizes positive, true and moral behavior.

More complete information concerning the nature of Bible texts, transmission of the texts, historical reliability of the Bible and other related topics can be found in the books listed in the Suggested Readings list.

Faith Builders

1. How does the Bible compare with other books in general? What about other religious books?

2. What influence has the Bible had on civilization? Is this usually what you hear about Christianity?

3. What does the unity of the Bible suggest about its origin?

4. What are some examples of Bible accuracy that you found interesting?

5. What are some evidences of inspiration of the Bible that you find especially significant?

Mountain Movers

Did the information in this chapter help strengthen your belief that the Bible is the true Word of God? Which evidence of the Bible as God's Word in this chapter was most convincing to you?

- Is your faith growing to the level that you can answer questions about God's Word confidently?

- Are you studying the Bible enough to equip yourself thoroughly for God's good work (2 Timothy 3:16-17)?

God has revealed all we need to know by giving us His Word, the Bible. He has made His will known to us. It is up to us to plant His Word in our hearts and grow a "mountain movers" type of faith. Is that possible? Yes! Remember Philippians 4:13: "I can do all things through Christ who strengthens me."

Some people are determined to prove that the Bible is not true. There are always skeptics who want to point out supposed "contradictions" in the Bible. When confronted with Bible passages that seem to contradict each other, consider the three factors below. Can you use these three factors to refute other supposed contradictions in the Bible?

1. *Is the same person or thing under consideration in both passages?* Example: If the ark was 450 feet long, 75 feet wide, and 45 feet high, how could men have picked up the ark and carried it? (Answer: The person is confusing two different arks: Noah's ark and the ark of the covenant.)

2. *Do the statements apply to the same time period?* Example: In Genesis 6:9, Noah is described as "a just man, perfect in his generations. Noah walked with God." In Genesis 9:21, Noah is drunk. How could Noah walk with God and be drunk? (Answer: The first description of Noah was given before the flood; Noah was drunk in his vineyard after the flood. Comments: Could Noah have continued to walk with God throughout his life, despite his human struggles? Do we? In Hebrews 11:7 and 13 Noah was described as a man of faith; the Bible says he died in the faith.)

3. *Is one author simply supplementing the other?* Just because one writer said something that adds to what another writer said about the same thing, that does not mean that he contradicted the other writer or that either writer made a mistake. Example: In Matthew 20:30-34, Jesus healed two blind men near Jericho. Mark 10:46-50 describes the same event, but says that Jesus healed a man called "blind Bartimaeus." (Answer: Matthew says two men were healed. Mark reports only one was healed. Taken together, it is evident that Jesus healed two blind men, one of whom was named Bartimaeus. Mark did not say Jesus healed only one man, and Matthew did not tell us the name of either man.)

Examining alleged contradictions in the Bible is not always easy. Depending on how severely someone is disagreeing with you, it may feel like you are up against a mountain that will not move! You may have to do some research and even then not be able to convince someone else that the Bible is right. It may contain some hard-to-understand passages, but no one has found any major contradictions. An important part of faith is our assurance that no matter what is questioned, the Bible is true. The Bible is from God, and it is God's gift to us. It is His plan to teach us how to grow and nurture our faith through His Word.

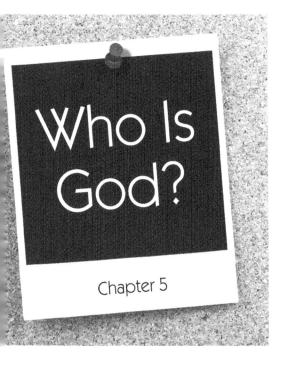

Who Is God?

Chapter 5

"Then Moses said to God, 'Indeed, when I come to the children of Israel … and they say to me, "What is His name?" what shall I say to them?' And God said to Moses, 'I AM WHO I AM.' And He said, 'Thus you shall say to the children of Israel, "I AM has sent me to you" ' " (Exodus 3:13-14).

Mustard Seed Moment

"Ninety-two percent of Americans say they believe in God, and 85 percent believe in heaven," according to a FOX News poll from September 2003 (Blanton). A poll by Harris Interactive taken at about the same time found that "79 percent of Americans believe there is a God, and 66 percent are absolutely certain this is true. Only 9 percent do not believe in God, while a further 12 percent are not sure" (Taylor).

It is obvious that something caused the creation of the universe and mankind. The only reasonable explanation is God. But why doesn't everyone believe in God? Why do some people say they believe in God but their lives paint a different picture?

Our God is truly an awesome God. Consider the way the human body is uniquely created. Could our solar system have happened by accident? God created the universe and everything in it in six days (Exodus 20:11). When He spoke, everything came into existence. God is able to move mountains; He is able to accomplish anything. Why would we not want our faith grounded in such an awesome God?

What do I do with a mustard seed? Power is revealed in the pages of His Word. Evidence that He is real comes from all directions. Our faith is what sets us apart, and believing is the seed that starts the process.

For our faith to grow, we must put God's Word into practice and see what a difference He can make in our lives and in the lives of those around us. In this chapter, we will study the Creator of the universe – our loving Father in heaven – and determine why He deserves our love, faith and obedience.

How Do You Describe God?

When asked what God is like, small children often reply something like, "He is a very old man with a long beard who lives somewhere up in the sky." Unfortunately, the concept of God that is held by many adults is not much better. Some people see God as a sort of Santa Claus who gives gifts to His children. Others see God as a policeman who enforces rules and prevents anyone from having any fun.

Who is God really? What is God like? These are not easy questions to answer. The Bible gives us some information about God – and although this information may not include everything we would like to know, it helps us understand some powerful things about God's nature and person.

What Can We Know About God?

We have available only two sources of information about God. The first of these is the natural world around us. As Paul eloquently advises in Romans 1:20, the universe itself reveals God's existence and creative activity. The majestic mountains, a beautiful sunset, a giant sequoia tree or a newborn baby – all point toward God. Actual details about God cannot be learned in this way, but the marvels of the natural world point toward God and provide us evidence that He is real.

Only in the Bible do we find specific details about God and His nature. This is really the only source of information we have. Details such as characteristics of God's nature, what He expects of us, and how we are to approach Him can be found only in the Bible. Limited though it may be, the information we have been given about God is sufficient for us to know that God exists, that we are His creation, that He wants to have a relationship with us, and what we need to do in response to Him.

The God of the Old Testament

In reading the Old Testament, we may think God seems distant and at times even frightening. He made Himself known as a pillar of fire, clouds with thunder and lightning, and a burning bush. He made Himself known to Abraham, gave the Law to Moses, and led the children of Israel out of Egypt.

In the Old Testament are three Hebrew words translated as "god" or "God" (*el, eloah* and *elohim*). The basic meaning of the words is "mighty one." These words are used to mean "God" as well as "god" or "gods," as in the gods of the Canaanites. But a proper name for God was used, too – a name given to Moses by God Himself at the burning bush. Out of reverence and respect, however, the Jewish people would neither speak nor write this name. Instead they substituted another name, which is usually translated as "Lord" in English translations of the Bible.

The Old Testament God was God of the children of Israel. The religion of the Israelites was monotheistic (recognized and worshiped only one god). This is in contrast to most other religions of the day, which were polytheistic (recognized and worshiped several gods). Throughout the Old Testament the emphasis is upon this one God, the God of Israel, who is to be worshiped and served to the exclusion of all other gods.

The God of Israel was definitely distinct from these other "gods" in the Old Testament and is described in various ways, including "almighty" (Genesis 17:1), "everlasting" (21:33), "jealous" (Exodus 20:5), "faithful" (Deuteronomy 7:9), "living" (Joshua 3:10) and "holy" (1 Samuel 6:20).

The God of the New Testament

In the New Testament the common Greek word *theos* was used for God. This word can refer to a god or God. The difference between the two meanings depends on the context. (See Acts 17:16-34 for Paul's explanation of this difference.)

The New Testament gives us much more information about God than the Old Testament. This is primarily because Jesus, God in the flesh, is the central character of the New Testament and the One who can truly "show us the Father."

Many images of God are found in the Old Testament, including that of a father. In the New Testament, however, the concept of God as the Father becomes most apparent. Jesus frequently referred to God in a personal way as "Father."

God as Creator

One of the most important concepts of the Bible is God as the creator of the physical universe. The Bible begins with this concept in Genesis 1:1, and it is a basic premise of the Christian faith (Hebrews 11:3). Christians assume or accept by faith that God created our world.

If this basic concept were not true, then all the rest of the Bible and the Christian faith would be worthless. Some believe this concept is outdated and that science has explained the origin of the universe by natural processes. In reality, however, even the best scientific theories are inadequate.

There are really only three possible explanations for the origin of the universe:

1. The physical universe has always existed.
2. The physical universe somehow originated out of nothing and has been shaped and formed into its present state by a series of random, chance events.
3. The physical universe was created by an intelligent, personal God.

Whichever you choose to accept will be a matter of faith. The question is, faith in what?

Other Characteristics of God

The Bible, especially the New Testament, contains specific information about God and His nature. In this section we will look at some characteristics of God to come to a better understanding of Him.

• **God is a spirit (John 4:24).** Jesus tells us that God is a spirit. A concept like that is not easy to understand because we are physical beings and confined by the limits of our physical existence. Some people believe the physical universe is all that exists. A basic concept of Christianity, however, is that a spiritual realm exists too and that God is a part of it. Belief in a spiritual realm opens up another dimension outside of the physical world we know. This will become even more important in a later chapter when we learn that we too have a spirit and that our spirit can live eternally with God.

• **God is light (1 John 1:5, 7).** As light contrasts with physical darkness, so God contrasts with spiritual darkness. The light of God illuminates our existence and helps us understand who we are and how we should live.

• **God is love (John 3:16; 1 John 4:7-11).** This is an absolute quality of God. We can understand love only in terms of God and how He loved us, especially in the giving of His Son to die for us and rescue us from our sinful natures.

• **God is holy (1 Peter 1:15-16).** Being holy, or set apart from other things, was important in the Old Testament. Although Christians do not have laws regulating holiness in the same manner as in the Old Testament, we still understand that God is holy and totally separated from all that is evil.

• **God is living (Hebrews 9:14).** Many "gods" have been known, but only one "living God" exists. We cannot prove this in any absolute sense. We do, however, have evidence of a living God in the physical universe, in the Bible, and in the lives of Christians who lived in the past and are living today.

• **God enters (John 1:1-5, 14; Galatians 4:4-5).** God entered the physical world as a human being. This is known as "the incarnation," which literally means to be "in-fleshed." We will look more closely at this concept in a later chapter and will see that this action was a necessary part of God's plan to bring mankind back into a relationship with Him that was severed by sin.

• **God gives (Romans 6:23; Ephesians 2:8-9).** God gives us grace – an unearned, undeserved gift. Without this gift no one can be saved. This gift is free to us, but it was bought at the terrible cost of the death of God's only Son.

• **God saves (Acts 2:38; Romans 8:1-2).** Only God can save us from our own sinful selves. In doing so, God reconciles us to Himself (Romans 5:6-11; Colossians 1:19-23) and removes the guilt of our sins through atonement (1 John 2:1-2). This is the result of the gift of God's grace and the sacrifice of His Son.

• **God listens (Matthew 7:7-12).** God has spoken to man through the ages in a variety of ways. In prayer we speak to God. Prayer is communication with God, based on the assurance that God will hear our prayers.

• **God re-creates (1 Corinthians 15:16-23).** This life is not all there is to existence. There is life beyond death and the grave. The next life is the resurrection, the only source of hope we have in the world. The basis of this hope was the resurrection of God's own Son, Jesus, and the promise that we too will someday be raised from the dead (Romans 6:1-14).

God as Three Persons

One of the most difficult things to understand about God is the concept of one God in three persons: God the Father, Jesus the Son and the Holy Spirit. This aspect of God is sometimes called the "Godhead." Actually, the word "Godhead" is found only in the New King James Version and the King James Version (Romans 1:20; Colossians 2:9). Other versions translate this word "Deity," "Divine Beings" or "Divine Nature."

Another term sometimes used to describe this aspect of God is the word "trinity." Although the word itself is not found in the Bible, it does describe this characteristic of God.

As we noticed earlier, Judaism was a monotheistic religion that worshiped a single God. Even so, it is interesting to note that one of the Hebrew words for "God" sometimes used in the Old Testament is actually plural (Genesis 1:26, for example). Some scholars believe this may be an early reference to God in three persons.

The New Testament refers to God as all three persons (Matthew 28:19; Ephesians 2:18; 1 Peter 1:2). Numerous references also are made individually to God, God as the Father, Jesus, Jesus as the Son, and the Holy Spirit.

In the next few chapters, we will examine in more detail the person and nature of Jesus and the Holy Spirit. In doing so we will learn more about God and His nature, especially as seen in Jesus and the Holy Spirit.

Faith Builders

1. What can we know about God from the physical world?

2. How did Paul describe the "unknown god" in Acts 17? Is this a description people can relate to today?

3. What is the significance of describing God as a spirit?

4. How is God light?

5. Which of the characteristics of God is most meaningful to you? Why?

Mountain Movers

It is not enough just to believe in God. As the survey noted in the "Mustard Seed Moment" at the beginning of this lesson, anyone can say they believe in God. If 92 or 79 percent (depending on which poll you believe) of Americans believe there is a God, why is our society as a whole so sinful?

- Is there a difference in belief and faith?
- If you met someone who did not believe in God, what are some reasons you could give to explain why you do believe in Him?
- What are some things that strengthen your belief that God is real?
- If someone asks you, "Where did God come from?", how will you answer?

Only in the Bible do we find specific details about God and His nature. The information the Bible gives us is sufficient for us to know that God exists, that He created everything including us, and that He wants us to have faith in Him and follow His commands.

God is our Creator and the master of the universe. God is the Father, the Son and the Holy Spirit in one. He deserves our highest love, honor and respect. Unfortunately, we don't always give Him what He deserves. Fortunately for us, God is forgiving if we are faithful.

- What kinds of things do people sometimes put before God? How important are sports, hobbies, entertainment, money and possessions? How does a person achieve the right balance?

- Think back to the Garden of Eden. What led up to Adam and Eve's sin?
- Satan tempted Eve to sin by speaking to her through a serpent. She and Adam decided to eat the forbidden fruit (Genesis 3:6). In what ways does Satan tempt us to make wrong decisions or to put other things before God today?
- God knows that we will not always make the right decisions, but He is a forgiving God. Satan is hard at work every day constantly tempting us in many ways (1 Peter 5:8-9). We must make the choice to follow God and have faith and confidence that He will help us through these trials and temptations in our lives.

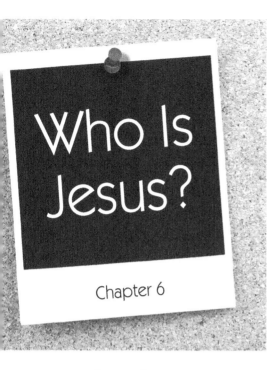

Who Is Jesus?

Chapter 6

"And suddenly a voice came from heaven, saying, 'This is My beloved Son, in whom I am well pleased' " (Matthew 3:17).

Mustard Seed Moment

In 2002, *Popular Mechanics* published an article titled "Real Face of Jesus" that displayed an updated artist's rendering of what Jesus may have looked like. By using methods similar to the ones police use in the field of forensic anthropology to solve crimes, scientists developed what they believed was the most accurate image of what Jesus would have looked like. The drawing shows Jesus as a brown-skinned man with short hair and a beard. But how is Jesus usually pictured in Bible story books and Bible illustrations? He is usually shown as a tall, thin, fair-skinned man with long hair and a beard. And he's usually wearing a white tunic with a blue sash. Is this how Jesus actually looked? Probably not. Some people believe that Jesus, as a hard-working carpenter's son, would not have been thin and fair-skinned but would have been muscular and tanned from working outside – that's pretty logical.

Jesus is probably the most well-known person ever to have lived, yet the Bible gives us very little physical description of Him. Isaiah 53:2b does say of Jesus' appearance that "when we see Him, There is no beauty that we should desire Him," indicating that His looks were nothing spectacular.

The magazine article noted that from what we know of history and genetics, if Jesus had the light-skinned features that we usually see pictured in Bible school literature, He "would have looked very different from everyone else in the region where [He] lived and ministered." Surely the authors of the Bible would have mentioned it if Jesus had looked drastically different from everybody else. In the Garden of Gethsemane, when Jesus was arrested before His crucifixion, "Judas had to kiss Jesus to indicate who He was, because apparently the soldiers could not tell him apart from his disciples." In reality, we can only speculate as to what Jesus might have looked like. The magazine article concludes that in the "absence of evidence, our images of Jesus have been left to the imagination of artists" (Fillon).

Ultimately, is it that important to know what Jesus looked like? In answering the question "Who Is Jesus?", there are more important things to consider than His physical appearance. The Bible reveals to us everything we need to know about Jesus from the time of His birth until the time He ascended to heaven to await the judgment.

What do I do with a mustard seed? Just as the mustard seed starts out small but grows to be greater than all herbs, Jesus came to earth as a newborn baby and grew to be a man greater than any other man who ever lived. In this chapter, we will learn that our belief in Jesus does not depend on what He looked like but rather on our faith in Him and the influence He has on our lives.

"Who Do You Say That I Am?"

Who is Jesus? The question is simple, but the answer may not be quite as simple. People often associate Jesus with various images they've seen during their lifetimes. For some people Jesus is the baby in the manger whereas others associate Him with the handsome, blue-eyed actor who portrayed Jesus in a particular movie. Others may see Jesus as a paper cutout placed on the flannelboard by a teacher long ago, or they remember Him as portrayed by their friend Johnny in the vacation Bible school play.

In Matthew 16:13-20, Jesus asked a similar question of His disciples: "Who do men say that I, the Son of Man, am?" Then, more pointedly, He asked, "Who do you say that I am?" This important question is one He still asks of us today.

Jesus Is Real

From time to time some people will claim that the stories of Jesus are mere myths or legends. However, ample evidence shows that this is not the case and that the Jesus we read about in the New Testament was a real person.

Most of what we know about Jesus comes from the Bible and the New Testament in particular. However, as we learned in earlier chapters, the Bible is a special book, and its claims, including those referring to Jesus, can be taken seriously.

Other references to Jesus are found outside the Bible. These references provide further evidence that Jesus was a real person and that details about Him in the Bible are neither myth nor legend. We will notice four examples taken from Ralph P. Martin's entry "Jesus Christ" in the *International Standard Bible Encyclopedia* (1034-1035). Additional information is available in the books listed in the Suggested Readings at the end of this book.

1. Suetonius was a Roman historian who was born in A.D. 69 and died sometime after 122. The following statement regarding certain events that had occurred is found in his writings: "Claudius expelled the Jews from Rome because of their continual quarreling at the instigation of Chrestus." The word "Chrestus" is very similar to "Christus," which is the Latin word for "Christ." For this reason many scholars believe this is a reference to Jesus. The statement is especially interesting in light of Acts 18:2, where Luke recorded that Claudius had expelled the Jews from Rome, probably referring to the same event.

2. Tacitus, a Roman historian who wrote around A.D. 115-117, referred to Christ, who was "put to death as a punishment during the reign of Tiberius at the hand of one of our procurators, Pontius Pilate." Tacitus recorded events related to the Roman Empire. Here he mentions Jesus and places Him in the same period of history as the New Testament. (See also Luke 3:1, which places Jesus in the time of these same Roman rulers.)

3. Pliny, who was governor of Pontus and Bithynia from A.D. 111 to 113, wrote a letter to the emperor, Trajan, requesting information on how to prosecute and punish those accused of being Christians. In this letter he refers to Christian believers meeting "before dawn on a set day and singing alternate verses to Christ as to a God." This letter con-

tains other interesting information about the early Christians, but this statement in itself provides evidence that Jesus was a person and that some believed Him to be divine.

4. Josephus, a Jewish historian who lived from A.D. 37 to 100, wrote about a man named Jesus who had been crucified by the procurator Pontius Pilate. Some portions of the statement by Josephus may not be original, but the passage still provides evidence that Jesus lived and that He was a real person.

None of these men were Christians or were in any way associated with the early church. They were simply recording or reporting information. Each of these examples does, however, point to Jesus as an actual, historical character and provides evidence that Jesus did in fact live.

Jesus Died and Rose Again

Jesus was crucified and placed in a tomb. These events are described in detail in the gospel accounts and mentioned in secular history as well. The gospels tell us, however, that He did not remain there. He rose from the dead and was seen by numerous individuals (1 Corinthians 15:3-8). Skeptics have attempted to deny the reality of the resurrection, but the New Testament writers give strong evidence for the historical authenticity of this event. The empty tomb, the reported appearances of Jesus after His resurrection, and the transformation of Jesus' disciples from panic and fear to bold proclamation of the news about the risen Lord all point to the reality of this event.

The risen Jesus still gives us hope for living, strength for going on when life presses us down, and courage to face death itself. In fact, without a resurrected Jesus, Christianity would be meaningless and Jesus Himself a fraud.

Jesus Will Come Again

Jesus returned to heaven after His resurrection, but He is coming back (John 14:1-4; Acts 1:1-11). He will return at the end of time (1 Thessalonians 4:13-18), but when He returns, Jesus will be the judge of all mankind (Matthew 25:31-46; Revelation 20:11-15).

Jesus Is the Son of God

We studied earlier that God exists in three persons, one of whom is Jesus, the Son. Various references in the New Testament identify Jesus as God's Son. On at least two occasions, God Himself spoke and referred to Jesus as His Son – at His baptism and at His transfiguration (Matthew 3:13-17; 17:1-6). Other references list Jesus separately from God the Father and the Holy Spirit (Matthew 28:18-20; 1 John 5:1-12).

Jesus Is Lord

The Greek word translated as "Lord" was commonly used as a form of respect, similar to "sir" in our language. Thus, in the gospel accounts when someone refers to Jesus as "Lord," the title may be more a sign of respect than an acknowledgment of Jesus as God.

This Greek word also could refer to a master, owner of a house, a legal guardian or someone with authority. Most important, it was the word used in the Greek translation of the Old Testament (the Septuagint) for the name of God. After the resurrection, the followers of Jesus understood more completely His divine nature. Thus, when the writers of the New Testament used the word "Lord" in reference to Jesus, they were aware of the full significance of the term. It would have been equivalent to calling Jesus "God."

Use of the word "Lord" in referring to Jesus is fairly rare in the gospels. In the remainder of the New Testament, however, use of the term "Lord" in reference to Jesus becomes more frequent and more significant. When Jesus is called "Lord" in the remainder of the New Testament, it carries a deeper reverence and respect.

We can see this, for example, at the conclusion of the first recorded sermon when Peter boldly proclaimed, "God has made this Jesus, whom you crucified, both Lord and Christ" (Acts 2:36). Later, when presenting this message for the first time to a non-Jewish audience at the house of Cornelius, Peter spoke of Jesus as the "Lord of all" (Acts 10:34-38).

Paul frequently used the term "Lord" when referring to Jesus in his writing. Two examples are especially significant: Ephesians 1:3-14 and Philippians 2:5-11. Some Bible scholars believe that both of these passages were originally a poem or hymn written to glorify Jesus. If this is the case, then these passages represent some of the earliest statements of faith in Jesus as Lord. Quite possibly, the early Christians who wrote these poems or hymns had themselves seen Jesus after His resurrection, or at least knew someone who had seen Him. Thus, these early poems are witness to the authority and lordship of Jesus by those who had seen and known Him.

Jesus Is Christ

We noted earlier that Jesus asked His disciples, "Who do you say that I am?" (Matthew 16:13-20). Peter's answer, "You are the Christ," was significant. The word "Christ" literally means "anointed" and is equivalent to the Hebrew word "Messiah." In the Old Testament three groups of people were anointed: prophets, priests and kings. God's anointed, the "Christ," filled all three roles.

For Jesus, "Christ" was more of a title than a name. The phrase "Jesus of Nazareth" was recognized as a name; it identified Him as a man named Jesus who was from Nazareth. "Jesus Christ" (literally, "Jesus, the Anointed One"), however, was more than a name because it indicated Jesus' relationship to God.

For the Jewish people, the term "Christ" or "Messiah" was filled with great meaning. It was the subject of Old Testament prophecies and expressed the expectations and hopes of the Jewish people. The "Christ" or "Messiah" also was the culmination of God's plan for His people.

The term "Jesus Christ" is found only four times in the gospels but is frequently applied to Jesus later in the New Testament ("Christ" or "Christ Jesus" also is used). Like the word "Lord," it came to be much more meaningful after the resurrection and was used more often in the remainder of the New Testament. There it expresses the relationship we have with Jesus: He is Lord, and He is Christ.

Jesus Is Our Savior

At the birth of Jesus, He was announced as the "Savior" of mankind (Matthew 1:20-21). In the Old Testament, predictions said He would suffer and die for others and receive the punishment and penalty that should have been our own (Isaiah 53:1-12). Those predictions were fulfilled in the death of Jesus on the cross. He was a sacrifice, much like the animals sacrificed under the Law of Moses, but He was the perfect and *final* sacrifice.

The concept of Jesus as Savior became the message of the first Christians (Acts 5:31; Philippians 3:20; 2 Timothy 1:8-10; 2 Peter 1:1; 2:20; 3:18). As they began to preach, their message was simple: Jesus had come, He died and was raised again, and salvation and forgiveness of sins are now available because of what Jesus did.

Faith Builders

1. How is the church itself evidence of Jesus' resurrection?

2. How did the disciples' view of Jesus change after the resurrection?

3. How many titles or words to describe Jesus can you name?

4. What was the message of the early Christians in regard to Jesus? Is this our message today?

Mountain Movers

If you had to describe Jesus to someone who had never heard of Him, what would be the first thing you would mention? Compare your answer with the answers of other class members. What are the most basic things about Jesus that a person needs to know?

In the "Mustard Seed Moment" of this chapter, it was noted how Jesus is generally pictured in Bible school literature. Do some research. Why is He usually shown as a tall, thin, fair-skinned, long-haired, bearded man wearing a white tunic with a blue sash? Did Jesus really have a halo or a bright light encircling His head? No. Investigate where the "halo" image originated. Share your findings with the class.

In Genesis 1:26, God said, "Let Us make man in Our image."

- How are we made in the image of God?
- What does the fact that God came to earth as a man prove about God's love for us?
- Because we are able to read about the life of Jesus in the Bible, what advantages do we have over those people who lived during Old Testament times?
- What advantages do we have over those people who lived during Jesus' lifetime on earth? Were they more faithful because they actually knew Him and saw His miracles firsthand?

Take another look at Genesis 1:26. Who is "Us"?

- Read Acts 17:24. Was God the Father there from the beginning?
- Read John 1:1-4, 14 and Colossians 1:13-17. Was Jesus the Son there from the beginning?
- Read Genesis 1:2. Was the Holy Spirit there from the beginning?

Jesus Christ is our Lord and Savior. What did you learn in this chapter about the significance of that statement? Specifically, what is important about Jesus as the Christ, Jesus as our Lord, and Jesus as our Savior?

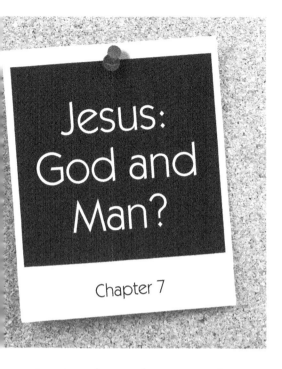

Jesus:
God and
Man?

Chapter 7

"And the apostles said to the Lord, 'Increase our faith.' So the Lord said, 'If you have faith as a mustard seed ...' " (Luke 17:5-6).

Mustard Seed Moment

An apple has three main parts: the peel, the flesh and the core. The peel is the thick outer covering that protects the apple from insects and disease. The flesh is the white part of the apple that tastes juicy and good. What happens to the flesh of an apple when the peel is removed? It soon begins to turn brown because it is no longer protected, right?

When Jesus came to earth, He left the protection of heaven behind. He came here to live among men, as a human being. Jesus shared His good part, His amazing life in the flesh, with us, but He was also hurt, bruised and beaten. Because He was God's Son and it was part of God's plan to save us from our sins, Jesus died, rose from the dead three days later and still lives today. We can have faith in Him and His existence from our confidence in the Scriptures.

Let's not forget the one last part of an apple – the core. The core is where the seeds are. The seeds are what guarantee that there will be more apples in the future. Where apple seeds are planted, new apple trees will grow. As a tiny mustard seed can grow into a large tree, a tiny apple seed can do the same. The heart or core of the apple is like the heart of Jesus. He should be the core of our faith.

What do I do with a mustard seed? In this chapter, we will learn that like a peeled apple, Jesus left His protective skin behind and came to earth in the flesh (as a man) to live, love and heal. He died in the flesh to save us from our sins, but because He was the Son of God, He arose and is still planting seeds of faith in our hearts today.

He Was One of Them

Jesus had gone back home to Nazareth, where He had grown up. On the Sabbath He went to the synagogue where He had sat each week as a child and a young man, and He began to teach. Mark recorded the reaction of the people: " 'Is this not the carpenter, the Son of Mary, and brother of James, Joses, Judas, and Simon? And are not His sisters here with us?' So they were offended at Him" (Mark 6:3). Their basic reaction was, "Who does He think He is? He's one of *us*!" Actually, they were right. He was one of them.

God in the flesh is not an easy concept to understand. As humans, understanding how we have both a physical body and a spirit is difficult enough. The idea of a spiritual being like God in a physical body is even tougher to grasp. Only in the person of Jesus can we see God in human form.

Jesus Was With God in the Beginning

The gospels give us many details about Jesus and His life and ministry. Matthew and Luke begin their accounts with the birth and genealogy of Jesus and His relationship with His human family. Mark begins with the ministry of Jesus and emphasizes Jesus as a teacher and worker of miracles. John, on the other hand, begins his gospel account not with Jesus the man but rather with Jesus as God (John 1:1-5). In the first two verses of his gospel, John makes this bold statement: "In the beginning was the Word, and the Word was with God, and the Word was God. He was in the beginning with God."

John used the term "the Word" to describe Jesus. The original word, *logos*, was a significant term in the Greek language. Professor and theologian Merrill C. Tenney writes in his commentary *John: The Gospel of Belief* that *logos* was used in Greek philosophy to denote "reason" or the "ultimate intelligence" that gave meaning to all things (62).

Scottish theologian William Barclay, in his commentary *The Gospel of John, Vol. 1*, points out that the term also would be recognized by

Jewish readers because in Jewish thinking, the Word of God was often personified (34). Thus, John sought to bridge the gap between Greek and Jewish thinking with Christianity through use of the term *logos*, or "the Word."

In these few verses we also see several important characteristics of Jesus. First, Jesus, the Word, was not a created being. He is eternal and was with God in the beginning. He existed before the creation. Not only was Jesus with God, but the "Word was God." In other words, Jesus is deity or one member of the Godhead. Thus, Jesus is one with God and is fully God in every aspect of His being.

Second, John 1:3 tells us, "All things were made through Him." As God, Jesus was involved in the creation. God with Jesus and the Holy Spirit formed everything that exists in our physical universe.

Finally, John tells us in 1:4 that "in Him was life." The verse is not only a reference to physical life. Although Jesus, along with God in the beginning, created physical life, John tells us the Word came in the flesh to give spiritual life as well (vv. 10-13).

The Word Became Flesh

Not only was the Word God and with God in the beginning, but the Word also became one of us. As John put it, "And the Word became flesh and dwelt among us" (John 1:14). This is known as the incarnation – God in the flesh.

Jesus, God's Son, was like you and me. He lived a life in the form of a human being. He was fully God, yet also fully man. As God in the flesh, Jesus experienced the full range of human emotions and physical sensations that we do. He experienced joy, happiness and excitement, but He also knew what it was like to be hungry, tired, sad or lonely.

Only by being both God and man could Jesus complete His task. He had to remain fully God to have the power to demonstrate His deity and conquer death, but He also had to be fully man to experience human existence.

In Galatians 4:4-5, Paul indicates that Jesus' coming in human form was a part of God's plan – He was sent by God in human form. Jesus experienced a physical birth and lived as a man. Not only did Jesus come to earth, but He also died as a sacrifice for our sins. Paul tells us that this too was a part of God's plan and was necessary to redeem us from our human weakness ("redeem" means "to buy back" as one would have bought a slave).

In Philippians 2:5-11, Paul reminds us that although Jesus was truly God, He put on the flesh of humanity to live and die a sacrificial death. This passage emphasizes that Jesus, "who, being in the form of God," also was "in the likeness of men." The whole purpose of Jesus coming to this world was not simply to live as we live but to die as a sacrifice for our sins.

He Died on a Cross but Was Raised Again

As a man, Jesus died and was buried, but Jesus as God was able to conquer death and rise from the dead. This was the same Jesus, the Christ, who was the fulfillment of prophecy and the One who demonstrated He was God's Son through miracles and His power over death.

This was the message the disciples of Jesus boldly proclaimed. They had seen the risen Lord, and their lives had been changed because of it. We can see this conviction in the first sermon after Jesus returned to heaven, recorded in Acts 2:22-40. Peter began his sermon by stating that Jesus came with power (v. 22), as was evident in the miracles He performed.

Even so, Jesus was rejected and nailed to a cross. His rejection was no accident, however; this too was part of God's plan (Acts 2:23; cf. 3:18; 4:28; 13:29.) Jesus was crucified and placed in a tomb, but God raised Him from the dead (vv. 24-35) and made Him Lord and Christ (v. 36).

Jesus as a man died and was nailed to a Roman cross, but Jesus as God conquered death in His resurrection. Only by being both God and man could Jesus accomplish this.

Jesus Can Relate to Us

Only as God and man could Jesus fully understand what it's like to be a human being. As God in the flesh, Jesus experienced every aspect of humanness. As God, this was not possible, but as man it was a very real experience for Him.

Various passages relate this concept. In Hebrews 2:17-18 we read that Jesus was like us in every way, even to the point of being tempted. This description reveals an important aspect of the incarnation: as God in the flesh, Jesus experienced what it was like to be human, even the temptation to sin. In this way He can relate to us as we struggle with sin in our lives.

Although tempted, Jesus was without sin, as is explained in Hebrews 4:14-16. This concept is important for at least two reasons. First, Jesus could have been the perfect sacrifice for our sins only if He had been sinless. And the fact that Jesus could live a sinless life provides encouragement to us as we try to live for God.

Faith Builders

1. Why is it so difficult to understand the concept of God in the flesh?

2. What does John 1:1-5 teach about "the Word"?

3. In what ways does Jesus give life?

4. What do Galatians 4:4-5 and Philippians 2:5-11 teach us about our relationship with God?

5. What does it mean to you to have a God who has lived as a man?

Mountain Movers

What elements of Jesus' ministry and mission have made the most difference in your life? What events that Jesus experienced during His life on earth compare to some of your life experiences?

- How can Jesus, who did not sin, possibly relate to us today who do sin?
- What part does our faith in Him play in that?
- What applications can we draw from what we read about Jesus' example in 1 Peter 2:21-24?

Review the details of Jesus' crucifixion and the events leading up to it, His death and resurrection given in Matthew 26–28, Mark 14–16, Luke 22–24, and John 18–21. Also review the account of His ascension in Acts 1:3-11. Included in these chapters are Jesus' final words to His disciples. How do the details of what Jesus endured and the fact that He did it to forgive our sins and provide a way for us to be saved affect you personally?

Sometimes we need to be reminded of the unfair and cruel death that Jesus suffered when He was God as a man here on earth. Many times we get so caught up in our day-to-day routines and busy lives that we forget the sacrifice God made in sending His Son to die on the cross for our sins.

Remembering His sacrifice and death on the cross in detail can help strengthen our faith. Knowing that He rose again and is coming soon (Revelation 22:20) should make us renew our faith in Him every day.

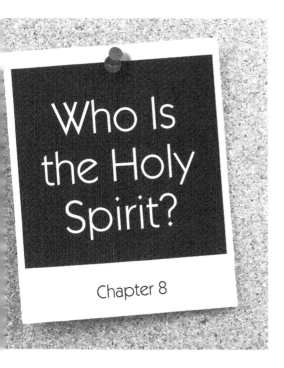

Who Is the Holy Spirit?

Chapter 8

"But the Helper, the Holy Spirit, whom the Father will send in My name, He will teach you all things, and bring to your remembrance all things that I said to you" (John 14:26).

Mustard Seed Moment

So far in this book, we have spent a great deal of time determining the characteristics of God and Jesus. But sometimes people have the most difficulty grasping the concept of the Holy Spirit – and how the Father, Son and Holy Spirit are one.

A simple illustration is water. It can be in the form of a liquid we drink from a glass. Water can also be frozen and become ice. It can also be boiled and become steam. But it is still water no matter its form – liquid, ice or steam. In the same way, God can be the Father, or in the form of Jesus the Son, or as the Holy Spirit, but He is still God.

A good way to aid in understanding how God works in this way is to imagine God, Jesus and the Holy Spirit on stage. From the beginning at Creation and throughout the Old Testament, God the Father was center stage. Jesus the Son and the Holy Spirit were there with Him, but God the Father was the One who communicated with the people. Later, in the Gospels of the New Testament and until He ascended, Jesus the Son was center stage. God and the Holy Spirit were still there with Him, but Jesus was the One who communicated with the people. Later in New Testament times and continuing until today, the Holy Spirit is center stage. God and Jesus are still with Him, but the Holy Spirit is God inside us working in our lives right now. We have the Bible to communicate stories and commands to build our faith and help us grow to be the Christians God wants us to be (Simmons 22).

What do I do with a mustard seed? In this chapter, we will examine what the Bible teaches us about the Holy Spirit and gain a better understanding of how He lives in those of us who are Christians, how that provides us a special relationship with God, and how living a faithful Christian life guarantees our salvation.

Physical Versus Spiritual

Christians believe each person has a spirit that makes up a part of his or her being. They also believe that God, Jesus and the Holy Spirit are spiritual beings. For humans to understand something spiritual in nature is not easy. Everything we know and experience is physical and confined to the physical limitations of our existence. Spiritual beings, on the other hand, are outside of the physical world and are, therefore, difficult for us to comprehend.

Also difficult for us to understand is the nature and role of the Holy Spirit. We can at least relate to God as a father and Jesus as a son, but understanding the Holy Spirit is more of a challenge, possibly because no human entity is equivalent in nature to the Holy Spirit. Nevertheless, the Holy Spirit is important to our understanding of God and the development of our Christian faith.

The Spirit of God in the Old Testament

The Hebrew word *ruah* can mean "breath," "wind" or "spirit." The word is used in a number of ways in the Old Testament, and the particular meaning of the word depends on the context in which it was used.

The word is sometimes used in the Old Testament to describe God's spirit, such as in these examples:

1. God's spirit was involved in the creation (Genesis 1:2).
2. God's spirit filled the judges who were chosen to lead the Israelites (Judges 3:10; 11:29).
3. God's spirit was given to David when he was anointed king (1 Samuel 16:13).
4. God's spirit inspired people to prophesy (1 Samuel 19:20).

One thing we can learn from these examples is that God's spirit was active and involved in various ways. As we will see later, this is a characteristic of the Holy Spirit in general.

The Holy Spirit in the New Testament

The Greek word *pneuma* also can mean "breath," "wind" or "spirit." Like the Hebrew word *ruah*, the particular meaning of *pneuma* is determined by its context.

In the New Testament the word "spirit" is used in several ways, including specific references to the Holy Spirit. Jesus, for example, associated Himself with God's Spirit when He identified Himself with the prophecy in Isaiah 61:1-3 (Luke 4:17-21).

Jesus also promised that the Holy Spirit would speak through the apostles (Matthew 10:19-20; Mark 13:11; Luke 12:11-12). This promise is especially evident in John's gospel, where several references are made to the Holy Spirit (called the "Helper" and "Spirit of truth" in the New King James Version, and the "Counselor" or "Comforter" in the New International Version). John recorded that Jesus promised specifically that the apostles would receive the Holy Spirit and that the Holy Spirit would guide them in their teaching (John 14:16-17; 16:13).

Other references to the Holy Spirit are found in the New Testament. We will notice some of these as we study further details about the Holy Spirit's nature.

The Holy Spirit Is a Person

Like God and Jesus, the Holy Spirit has a personality and the attributes or characteristics of a person. Some of these include:
1. judgment (Acts 15:28-29);
2. mind (Romans 8:26-27);
3. an ability to determine certain things (1 Corinthians 12:11); and
4. emotions (Romans 15:30; Ephesians 4:30).

The Bible also indicates that the Holy Spirit performs certain tasks. The Holy Spirit:
1. teaches and reminds (John 14:26);

2. guides (John 16:13);
3. speaks (Acts 8:29; 11:12); and
4. intercedes (Romans 8:26-27).

Although we may have difficulty envisioning the Holy Spirit as a person, we can see from these examples that the Holy Spirit has capabilities and actions similar to those of a person. We also can see from these references that the Holy Spirit is active and involved in various aspects of God's interaction with mankind.

The Holy Spirit and Christians

The exact relationship between the Holy Spirit and Christians today is sometimes a source of misunderstanding and confusion because the role of the Holy Spirit in the life of Christians has changed since the very beginning of the church.

A study of that role can be divided into three areas: baptism of the Holy Spirit, miraculous gifts of the Holy Spirit, and the indwelling of the Holy Spirit.

Baptism of the Holy Spirit

The "baptism of the Holy Spirit" was a special situation in which certain individuals received miraculous powers from the Holy Spirit. Such bestowing of power is recorded only two times in the New Testament and, therefore, we assume it was limited in nature.

This baptism of the Holy Spirit had been predicted by prophets, such as Joel (Joel 2:28-29; Acts 2:16-21). John the Baptist and Jesus also had predicted this baptism (Matthew 3:11; Acts 1:5).

As far as we can determine from the Bible, the baptism of the Holy Spirit was given only to two groups of people. These were the apostles on the Day of Pentecost (Acts 2:1-13), and Cornelius and others in his house when Peter preached to them about Jesus (Acts 10:24-48).

In writing about these events in Acts, Luke is very specific about what actually took place. In the case of the apostles in Acts 2, he identifies (1) the sound of a rushing wind, (2) the appearance of tongues that resembled fire, and (3) the ability of those receiving the Holy Spirit to speak other languages. When a similar event occurred at the home of Cornelius, several people began speaking in other languages (Acts

10:44-48). Peter and those with him recognized the similarity to the event on Pentecost and realized God had given the Holy Spirit to these individuals as well.

What was the purpose of the baptism of the Holy Spirit? In the case of the apostles, its purpose was to guide and instruct them in God's Word (John 14:26; 16:13). No written documents other than the Old Testament existed for reference, so God gave them direct information. As a result, the apostles began immediately to preach and teach about Jesus. They also served as the early leaders in the church and wrote portions of the New Testament under the influence of the Holy Spirit.

The baptism of the Holy Spirit at the house of Cornelius, on the other hand, seems to have been a demonstration of God's intent to allow the Gentiles to become a part of His church along with the Jews. Both events were significant. The first marked the opening of the doors of the new kingdom to the Jews, and the second marked the opening of the kingdom to the Gentiles.

Miraculous Gifts of the Holy Spirit

Through the baptism of the Holy Spirit, the apostles received miraculous gifts as well as the ability to pass on certain gifts to others through the laying on of their hands (Acts 8:14-17; 19:1-6). Only the apostles possessed this ability, and it was limited to that period of time. The effect was to allow others to receive miraculous gifts (1 Corinthians 12:1-11; Ephesians 4:11-13), which enabled the early Christians to receive revealed knowledge from God and also to demonstrate God's power as they performed miracles. An example can be seen in Acts 8:5-8, where Philip went into Samaria teaching, healing and performing other miracles.

These abilities, however, were temporary and ended with those who had received this gift directly from the apostles. Since the completion of the New Testament, this power has been replaced by the written Word (1 Corinthians 13:8-10). We now have God's complete revelation ("that which is perfect has come") and no longer need these specialized gifts of the Holy Spirit.

Indwelling of the Holy Spirit

The third role of the Holy Spirit in relation to Christians is one of "indweller." The indwelling of the Holy Spirit is a gift, promised to all Christians, that accompanies obedience and baptism (Acts 2:37-38; 5:32).

This gift provides all Christians with a special relationship with God but does not impart miraculous powers. The gift of the Holy Spirit is a guarantee of our salvation (Ephesians 1:13-14). The Holy Spirit also gives us access to God (2:11-22) as well as strength and assistance in certain situations (Romans 8:1-27; Ephesians 3:14-21).

Faith Builders

1. Describe how you perceive the Holy Spirit.

2. How would you summarize the works of the Holy Spirit?

3. In what two ways were miraculous gifts of the Holy Spirit received in the book of Acts? How did these ways differ?

4. What was the purpose of the baptism of the Holy Spirit and the miraculous gifts of the Holy Spirit? Are these still necessary today?

5. How would you describe the indwelling of the Holy Spirit in a Christian today?

Mountain Movers

Spiritual beings are sometimes difficult to understand. The Holy Spirit is referred to in Scripture as a "He," not an "it." The Holy Spirit has a personality. This chapter discussed many aspects of our understanding of the Holy Spirit according to what we learn in the Bible.

In review, the gift of the Holy Spirit that we receive at baptism is not the same as the gift of the Holy Spirit we read about in the early New Testament. The apostles were given the ability to perform miracles so that people would believe. Today, we have God's Word to tell us of these events. Miraculous gifts are no longer needed.

- Have you ever talked with a person who believes in faith-healing today – such as televangelists who claim to make lame people walk?

- Have you ever had a conversation with a person who believes he or she can speak in tongues?
- Can you see why Bible study is so important to determine what is true or not true today?

We receive the gift of the Holy Spirit when we are baptized (Acts 2:38). The Holy Spirit gives all Christians a special relationship with God, but He does not give us miraculous powers.

The Holy Spirit helps us to be spiritually minded. Sin begins as a seed in the mind. It is a work of the Holy Spirit to help us control our mind and thoughts.

- How can we do our part to keep our minds clean? Consider your favorite TV shows or movies. What sites do you frequent on the Internet? All of us are usually guilty at times of falling into the worldly trap for the sake of comedy, adventure or entertainment. How much time do we spend in front of the television or on the computer each day? How could our time be better spent?

The Holy Spirit in our lives can help us win the fight against sin and help us overcome our weaknesses and temptations. God's love and promised forgiveness will help us keep on track.

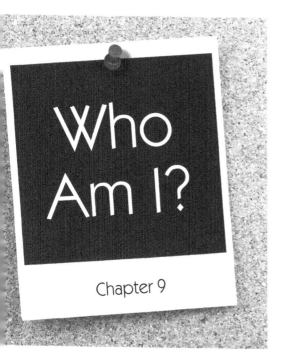

Who Am I?

Chapter 9

"God created man in His own image; in the image of God He created him; male and female He created them. Then God blessed them, and God said to them, 'Be fruitful and multiply; fill the earth and subdue it; have dominion over the fish of the sea, over the birds of the air, and over every living thing that moves on the earth' " (Genesis 1:27-28).

Mustard Seed Moment

Were the people first mentioned in the Bible intelligent? Yes. Although Adam and Eve made the sinful choice to listen to Satan, the Bible clearly shows that they could think, talk, take care of the garden and make decisions. They even thought they could hide from God!

In Genesis 4:21, Jubal is described as the "father of all those who play the harp and flute." In verse 22, Tubal-Cain was "an instructor of every craftsman in bronze and iron." These were talented and intelligent men. Noah built an ark carefully following God's blueprint. Although they had the wrong motives, it took people of intelligence and skill to build the Tower of Babel. From the beginning, the Bible proves that God made us intelligent beings.

What do I do with a mustard seed? In this chapter, we will learn that the most important aspect of being human is that we can have a personal relationship with God. We were created in God's image, and He wants us to use our minds to study diligently and grow our faith in Him.

Finding Our Place in the World

Who am I? Where did I come from? When we ask questions like these, we are often seeking to find some meaning in our existence or some place for ourselves in the vastness of the universe.

Evolutionary theories are little help because they tell us we are merely animals – highly evolved animals, but still just animals. They provide little in the way of answers to the question, "Who am I?" Based upon a naturalistic view of the world, these theories assume that physical matter is all that exists, that life formed spontaneously from nonliving chemicals, and that all living things, including human beings, have developed through evolutionary processes. Human characteristics such as personality, intelligence or creativity are explained as merely the result of chemical and physical processes. Even the human tendency to worship something beyond ourselves is explained away in naturalistic terms.

For the Christian, God has given meaningful answers to such questions about our existence. Based upon what God has revealed in His Word, we can know where we came from, why we are here, and where we are going. We must accept these answers by faith, of course. In reality, however, we have two choices: either we place our faith in a personal, intelligent Creator, or we place our faith in an impersonal, unguided series of chance events. The choice is ours.

The Creation Account

Genesis 1 and 2 contain what is called the creation account, in which a very brief summary of God's activities is written in nonscientific language. Even so, it gives us the information we need to understand where we came from and our place in the world around us.

In the original language of Genesis, two different words were used to describe God's activities. Both of these words describe God's act of creating, but they indicate different types of activity. The first word is translated "created" and is found in Genesis 1:1; 1:21; and 1:27 (see also 5:1-2). The specific creative acts of God are:

1. the initial creation out of nothing (1:1);
2. the creation of conscious life, or animals (1:21); and
3. the creation of man (1:27).

The wording in these verses suggests that these three actions were separate and distinct from other creative activity. Also, a special emphasis on the word "create" is implied in Genesis 1:27 and 5:1-2. In both cases, when the word "create" is used in reference to humans, it is repeated three times – apparently a way to emphasize that God had created human beings.

The remainder of the creation account emphasizes other aspects of God's activity. Genesis 1:2, for example, indicates that God also began to shape and form, or differentiate, the initial creation He had brought into existence. This action also can be seen in the second type of creative activity, which is designated by the phrase "let there be," found, for example, in 1:3, 6, 9 and 14. The original word for this phrase implies further shaping of the initial creation. Here God is forming, shaping and arranging what He had made into what we see in the world today, such as the sun, moon, stars, sea, land and plants.

The Creation of Humans

Two important passages in Genesis help us understand our status as human beings. The first is Genesis 2:7, which teaches that humans were formed "of the dust of the ground." Our physical bodies are made of the same material as the earth and other living things. The atoms and molecules that make up our bodies are the same as those that make up the rest of the universe.

The passage also teaches that when God formed the first man, He "breathed into his nostrils the breath of life; and man became a living being." Some versions translate "living being" as "living soul," which has led to some misunderstanding. "Living being" is much closer to the original idea expressed in the Hebrew word.

The term "breath of life" is used in reference to animals as well as humans (Genesis 7:21-22). Thus, the "breath of life" is not unique to humans. The "breath of life" appears to be that which gives physical life and makes our bodies alive in the same way that animals are alive. We might think of this as "biological life." It is also the part of our human nature that ceases to exist in physical death.

We should not be surprised, then, that our cellular makeup, physiological processes and genetic makeup are very similar to that of animals and other living things. This fact does not make us any less human but does remind us that a part of us is made of "dust" and that we share some things with the rest of the physical world.

The second important passage is Genesis 1:26-27. In these verses, the two crucial terms are "image" and "likeness." Humans were created in the "image" and "likeness" of God, which makes us special and sets us apart from the rest of the creation. Only humans are made in God's image and bear His likeness. "Likeness" here does not seem to refer to a physical characteristic because there is nothing physical about God. The "image" and "likeness" of God, therefore, must be in reference to our spiritual nature.

What Does It Mean to Be Human?

Of all the creatures that have ever lived on earth, only humans bear the "image" and "likeness" of the Creator. This makes us different and unique, and is reflected in our human nature, which is very different from that of animals. This uniqueness reveals itself in several ways:

• **Humans have personality.** Only humans can form a personal relationship with other human beings and with God Himself.

• **Humans are religious.** From the earliest records of human activity, we see some form of worship and regard for something outside of the physical world.

• **Humans are creative.** Only humans have been able to produce art, music, literature, architecture, science and technology.

• **Humans are conscious of time.**

• **Humans are able to comprehend the concepts of the future and the past.**

• **Humans have a moral nature.** All human cultures that have been studied have possessed some standard of moral or ethical behavior.

Human beings are different from all other created beings. American theologian and philosopher Francis Schaeffer called this difference "mannishness" and suggested that it is the result of bearing the image and likeness of God. When God created man, He created a special creature with certain "God-like" characteristics.

Have There Been Other "Humans"?

We sometimes hear about discoveries of "human ancestors." What are these, and how do they relate to the book of Genesis? First, we need to understand that these discoveries are fossils, or bones that have been preserved in rocks. Usually these fossils are very fragmentary and do not represent a complete skeleton. As such, these remains are "reconstructed" based upon certain presuppositions, the primary one being that humans have evolved from lower forms of life.

These fossils often have some physical resemblance to human beings, such as the shape or arrangement of bones. It seems probably, however, that most of these fossils came from ape-like creatures rather than human beings created in the image of God.

The Relationship Between God and Human Beings

The most important aspect of being human is our ability to have a personal relationship with the God who created us. This relationship is the result of being created in the image and likeness of God. Human beings are similar in many ways to other living things, but only humans have a spiritual dimension and an inner spirit that enable us to have a personal relationship with God Himself.

Faith Builders

1. What are the two types of "creative activity" we read about in Genesis 1 and 2? Which of these is used to describe the creation of man and woman?

2. What is the "breath of life," and how does it relate to us as humans? What does it tell us about our relationship with the rest of the creation?

3. What does it mean to be human? How would you define a human being?

4. Why do we often fail to live up to the "image" and "likeness" God has given us?

Mountain Movers

In this chapter, the statement was made that God has given meaningful answers to questions about our existence. We have a purpose in being here. Based on what God told us in the Bible, how would you answer these questions?

- Where did we come from?
- Why are we here?
- Where are we going?

Do you believe your life is just a series of chance events, or do you believe God has a plan for your life? How can you know what that plan is?

Review the creation story in Genesis 1–3. Re-emphasize in your mind the importance of a Creator who knew what He was doing and had a plan.

- God made us in His image. Why is that important?
- What conversation would you have with a person who believes in the theory of evolution?
- What conversation would you have with a person who does not believe God exists?
- Because we are human, we have the ability to have a personal relationship with God. How strong is your personal relationship with Him? What can you do to strengthen your relationship?

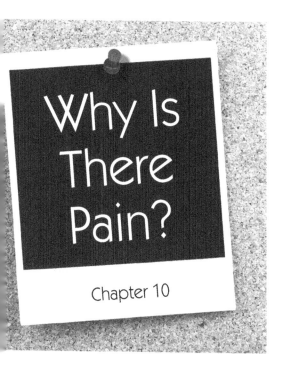

Why Is There Pain?

Chapter 10

" 'For My thoughts are not your thoughts, Nor are your ways My ways,' says the LORD" (Isaiah 55:8).

Mustard Seed Moment

A man dreamed he was in a place with two fine and fancy banquet rooms. In the first room, a banquet table was piled high with the most wonderful foods imaginable. However, everyone sitting at that banquet table was thin, sickly and starving. It was a terrible sight to see so much food going to waste. Then the man discovered a weird quirk. None of the people in this room could bend their elbows! They couldn't feed themselves, so they were starving! All that great food was just sitting there, and no one could eat it!

In the second banquet room was another table piled high with the same wonderful foods. But in this room, everyone was sitting around the table, happy, feasting and enjoying each other's company. The man discovered the same weird quirk he had noticed in the other room. These people could not bend their elbows either, but these people were all eating. How? Because they could not bend their elbows, these people couldn't feed themselves – but they had discovered that they could feed each other!

"Why do we have to suffer?" and "Why is pain in the world?" are difficult questions to answer. But our times of weakness can be times of strength. God tells us that even in our suffering we can help others. Just as the people in the second banquet room discovered they could help each other, we may discover that we have endured similar trials that someone else is now suffering. In helping others, we can help ourselves.

Satan causes the pain and suffering in this world. He wants to try anything and everything to make us lose faith and turn from God. And he is really good at his job. Why does God allow so much pain and suffering? Sometimes there is no good answer.

What do I do with a mustard seed? In this chapter, we will investigate what the Bible says about pain and suffering. We will learn that we need to develop a trust in God and have faith that He will take care of us – no matter how bad it gets, no matter what happens in our lives. Will we let Satan gain control of us in our tough times? Or will we have faith in God who has promised to establish and settle us even in our suffering (1 Peter 5:10)?

Real Life Has Real Pain

For as long as I can remember, the poor coyote in the *Looney Tunes* cartoons has been trying to catch the roadrunner. In trying to do so, he has been blown to bits; smashed by boulders; run over by cars, trucks, buses and trains; and fallen off too many cliffs to count. Each time, however, he appears to be unscathed from the ordeal and ready to mount a new attack. Unfortunately, real life is not like this cartoon world. In real life, many things hurt. Pain, disease, suffering and death are a real part of our world.

Events in our lives, over which we may have no control, can leave us hurting. Illness, the death of a grandparent, family financial problems, the divorce of our parents, a friend on drugs, or any number of physical, emotional or even spiritual traumas can bring pain into our lives. These may leave us with feelings of fear, anxiety, helplessness, and even hopelessness and despair.

If by some chance we have escaped pain in our lives, then we need only look around us to see that we live in a world of suffering. It is not hard to find someone hurting. We need only look in our neighborhood, at school, at work or at church, or to read the newspaper or watch the evening news. Pain is universal. It has transcended all social, economic and political boundaries. Pain is no respecter of persons.

Is pain an obstacle to faith? It can be. Understanding pain and suffering, however, can lead us to faith rather than away from it.

A World of Hurting

Pain and suffering in an individual's life can cause the person to ask questions such as, "Why me?" "What have I done to deserve this?" or "Why did God do this to me?" The suffering of other innocent people also can cause a person to ask similar questions or even have doubts about the goodness of God. Where can we turn for help?

Science can offer little help other than describing the biological process of pain or providing medications to dull the pain. Philosophy and other human intellectual pursuits are likewise of little help. Many people turn to religion in times of hurting. Other than Christianity, however, most religions believe all events are predetermined by fate and see suffering as inevitable.

Only in Christianity and the person of Jesus can any hope be found for those who are hurting. Early in His ministry, Jesus identified Himself with the suffering of this world, and much of His ministry was given to healing those who were hurting (Luke 4:16-21). We no longer can touch and heal as Jesus did, but the message of Christianity is still one of healing, hope and comfort (2 Corinthians 1:3-4).

Christianity is not, however, a vaccine to make one immune from pain or suffering. Some people may believe naively that when a person becomes a Christian, God will then bless him or her with a life free of pain, anxiety, sorrow or unhappiness. Such is not the case. Christians hurt just like everyone else. The message of Christianity, however, is hope. Through God's compassion and comfort and the power of Jesus' resurrection, Christians can overcome pain, suffering, illness and even death itself.

What Is Pain?

The word "pain" actually comes from a word meaning "penalty." Generally, we consider pain to be something negative. For most of us the experience of pain is something to be avoided if at all possible. This can be seen in the array of pain relievers available today. No one wants a headache, even for a little while.

Pain is also something we often fear. This is especially true of continuous or excruciating pain associated with certain injuries or illnesses. Biologically, pain is the response of the body to some injury or disease

– a signal from the nervous system that something is wrong. The bottom line is that pain hurts.

Pain is necessary for life, however. The thought of a world without pain is certainly pleasant, but physical existence without pain would be impossible. Although rare, some people are born without the capacity for feeling physical pain. Others lose the sensation of pain because of certain disease conditions. In either case, life is difficult for such a person. Injuries or infections can go unnoticed because the signal of pain is missing.

Pain is unpleasant for a reason. It is a signal, and if pain were not unpleasant, then it would be easy to ignore that signal. Pain is necessary for survival and is a part of God's design for animal and human existence.

As humans we experience different types of pain. Physical pain results when nerve impulses from pain receptors are received and interpreted by the brain. Often this is known as acute pain. Acute pain generally lasts only a short time and can result from a scraped knee or a stomachache. Physical pain also can be chronic. Chronic pain lasts for a long period of time – months or even years – and is generally associated with certain diseases or conditions. Chronic pain is much more difficult to live with than acute pain.

We as humans also experience emotional pain. Emotional pain is different from physical pain but is no less real. Many things can cause a person to hurt emotionally, and often these pains are more difficult to understand or endure than physical pain.

Pain and Suffering in the Bible

Someone unfamiliar with the Bible might believe it has very little to do with pain or suffering. The Bible, however, is a book written by humans about some very real human problems and needs. Aside from their inspiration by the Holy Spirit, the writers of the Bible were ordinary people.

The assumption probably could be made that the writers of the Bible were even more familiar with pain, suffering and death than we are today. Very few medicines were available then, and what medical care might have been available was expensive. Death was common. Infant mortality was high. Disease and death easily could sweep through a community. No hospitals or nursing homes existed to care for the sick.

It should come as no surprise, then, that numerous references to pain and suffering appear in the Bible. In both the Old Testament and the New Testament, several words or phrases are used to refer to pain, suffering and illness. In the Old Testament, for example, we find various terms for physical and emotional pain (Job 33:19; Jeremiah 15:18; 51:8). Other words in the Old Testament refer to sadness, sorrow, grief, and specific conditions such as blindness, lameness and paralysis.

In the New Testament are various words that have been translated as "distress," "grief," "sorrow," "pain" and "painful" (John 16:6, 20-22; Romans 9:2; 2 Corinthians 2:1, 3; 7:10; Philippians 2:27; Hebrews 12:11; 1 Peter 2:19). A word for "suffering" is found in the New Testament (Mark 5:26; Luke 17:25; Acts 17:3; Hebrews 13:12) as well as other words used to describe specific illnesses and diseases (Matthew 10:8; Luke 7:21-22; Acts 3:2; 8:7; 9:33; 12:21-23).

Pain and suffering played a very real role in the lives of those in Bible times. This is evident from the variety and number of words used in the Bible to refer to pain or illness. The subject matter of the Bible also reflects the importance of this topic. The book of Job and many of the Psalms, for example, deal specifically with problems of faith associated with pain and suffering. This connection also can be seen in the importance given to the healing ministry of Jesus and the apostles, and through the lives of other individuals such as the man who desired to be healed at the Pool of Bethesda (John 5:1-15) and the men who persisted in bringing their paralyzed friend to Jesus (Mark 2:1-12).

Faith Builders

1. What effects can the existence of pain and suffering in the world have on a person's faith?

2. What is pain? Why is pain necessary? What would life be like without pain?

3. What are some typical responses of people when they experience pain in their lives?

4. Did the writers of the Bible have a realistic view of pain and suffering?

5. Does living a life based on faith provide any comfort in times of suffering?

Mountain Movers

Pain and suffering were evident in the lives of many people we read about in the Bible. Jesus spent a great deal of His time on earth helping those who were in pain and healing those who were hurting.

- Has pain ever been an obstacle to your faith or to the faith of someone you know?
- Do we hurt any less because we are Christians?
- Discuss some specific instances of people in Bible times who suffered pain. How did they handle it? What comfort can that give us in trying to overcome our suffering? How can the way God helped these people through their pain help us trust Him more?

For most of us, pain is something we try to avoid. However, as we learned in this chapter, physical existence in this world without pain would be impossible. An important point we learned was that pain is unpleasant for a reason. If it didn't hurt, it would be easy to ignore. What is important about recognizing our pain?

- Emotional pain is different from physical pain. Can you give some examples to prove that statement?
- Remember the story in the "Mustard Seed Moment" about the people feeding each other. What are some sufferings you have experienced that have resulted in you being able to help others?

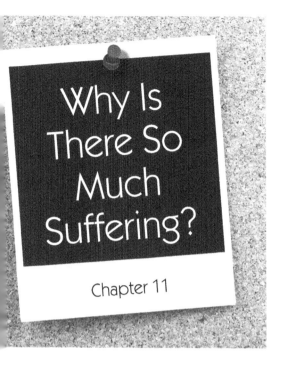

Why Is There So Much Suffering?

Chapter 11

"Naked I came from my mother's womb, And naked shall I return there. The LORD gave, and the LORD has taken away; Blessed be the name of the LORD" (Job 1:21).

Mustard Seed Moment

Sept. 11, 2001, rocked our world.

About 3,000 people died that day from two hijacked planes crashing into the World Trade Center towers in New York City and the subsequent collapse of those buildings; from a plane crashing into the Pentagon; and from another plane that crashed near Shanksville, Pa., after being detoured from its original target, believed to be the White House or the U.S. Capitol building in Washington, D.C.

That day was a tragedy on a major scale, but we all have pain and sufferings we endure throughout our lives. Ours may not be as dramatic as what happened Sept. 11, 2001, but let's face it – pain and suffering hurt. We know that. Most of us have had close family members die, some perhaps through disease or terminal illness, some in accidents. Many of us have seen the effects of alcohol and drug abuse; we have wrecked cars, broken up relationships, and experienced traumatic events. Sometimes this world is not easy. We have all had to endure tough times for one reason or another.

What do I do with a mustard seed? The question has been asked, "Why do bad things happen to good people?" Or even, "Why do bad things happen to God's people?" In this chapter, those questions will be investigated. Christians need to realize that nothing in this life is permanent. God didn't create us to stay on earth forever. Especially in the tough times, our faith in God is sometimes the only thing we can cling to that helps us make any sense out of what His plan is for our lives.

We Can't Help But Ask "Why?"

Our media-dominated society makes it especially difficult to escape from bad news, even for a short time. Wars, natural disasters, drunk drivers, terrorism, random snipers, disease, poverty – we seem unable to escape from the conclusion that we live in a world filled with pain and suffering. Any thinking person will sooner or later ask, "Why?"

What about God? How does He enter into the picture of pain and suffering? For many these questions become serious issues related to faith. Someone may ask, "If there is an all-powerful, loving and kind God, why does He allow pain and suffering in the world?" Such questions come from the very heart and soul of our existence, and we long for meaningful answers.

Christians are no different from others in their search for these answers. We hurt and see others hurting, and we want to know why. Although no easy answers are evident, being a Christian and understanding the true nature of our existence may help us come to terms with these questions.

What Might Have Been

God could have created a perfect world of perfect beings. He could have created an environment without pain, illness or even death. We would have been, however, little more than desensitized robots, incapable of any feeling and programmed to carry out some predetermined existence.

Instead, God created us as conscious beings, capable of feeling not only pain, sorrow and sadness, but also joy, happiness and love. Along with these capabilities God gave us responsibilities. He created us with the power of choice (Genesis 2:15-17; 3:1-7).

Much of the pain and suffering in the world is caused by wrong choices. Many people put the blame on God when it should be on them. Such wrong choices can be summarized in one word: sin. The Bible teaches that the consequences of sin are ultimately spiritual, but sin also has other serious consequences. Alcoholism, drug abuse, and the acquiring of a sexually transmitted disease, for example, all begin with a choice – and making the wrong choice can lead to pain and suffering.

What About Diseases?

Where did diseases come from? Many people believe that disease is punishment from God. In the book of Job, this was the basic idea of Job's friends. They essentially said to Job, "God punishes sin. You are being punished. Therefore, you must have sinned." The disciples also voiced this opinion in John 9:1-2 when they asked Jesus who had sinned to cause the man to have been born blind.

God at times has used plagues or diseases to punish people, but in each case it was clearly specified that this was a special situation and that God was sending the disease or plague as a form of punishment. No evidence in the New Testament supports the idea that God regularly does this today.

Diseases generally originate from three primary causes. Many diseases are caused by germs – usually bacteria or viruses that are known to cause specific diseases. Some diseases are caused by genetic or environmental factors, and still others are caused by physical factors such as malnutrition or even stress.

In other words, diseases are caused by factors within the natural world. We do not know if any diseases were a part of the world when God created it. We do know, however, that our current world is scarred by sin and that disease is a part of that world.

Physical Laws of the Universe

We live in an orderly universe governed by natural laws. Science has learned much about these laws and how they maintain our world. We can use these laws, for example, to explain the motion of planets or why your soup gets cold while you are talking on the phone. By manipulating these laws we can make cars go and airplanes fly. Yet these same laws can cause people to be injured or even lose their lives in car accidents or plane crashes.

Consider gravity as an example. Gravity is necessary for the motion and position of planets, revolution of the earth, seasons, tides and other natural processes. Gravity is necessary for our existence on earth. However, it also can be the cause of serious injuries and natural disasters.

The laws of nature cause earthquakes, floods, tornadoes, and volcanic eruptions. Are these really natural "disasters"? If an earthquake or volcanic eruption occurs in an isolated part of the earth, we think of it as a natural geological process. If an earthquake occurs in an urban area, however, it becomes a "natural disaster."

The laws of nature also can be used for evil purposes. The same technology used to make surgical instruments can also make guns and bombs. The same chemical laws used to make medicines to save lives can be used to make drugs that can lead to addiction and destroy lives.

Life Is Not Fair

I noticed a bumper sticker one day that read, "Life is hard, and then we die." Although very pessimistic, this describes the world in which we live. There are lots of "hard things" in life, many of which we do not understand. Doesn't God know about this? Why doesn't God terminate evil and wickedness?

Certainly God knows about such things. To make a perfect world, however, God would have to eliminate the freedom of choice He has given to us or violate the natural laws of the universe. Doing so would reduce us to robots living in an environment controlled by the whims of some outside force.

We are not the first to raise such questions about life. Read Psalm 73, paying particular attention to verses 1-5, 12-14 and 16-17. Here we are presented with the thoughts of a hurting person. He has seen the injustice in the world and cannot understand why God allows life on earth to be that way. His conclusion is really quite simple: Life is unfair, and sometimes evil people prosper and innocent people suffer, but God will eventually make things right.

God Will Be With His People

Yes, life can be difficult, but God has promised to be with us. God does not promise to take away pain, and He does not promise a life without problems. God does, however, promise to be with His people always.

In Romans 8:28 we read that God promises to remain with His people no matter what happens. This promise can give us hope in a world of suffering. Whether it's good times, bad times, happiness, sorrow, pain or grief, God is always there. God is the only certain thing in an uncertain existence.

God Is Not Merely a Spectator

A spectator sits in the stands and watches the game. God, however, is not merely a spectator; He is a participant. John wrote, "And the Word became flesh and dwelt among us" (John 1:14). Jesus lived as a man. He understands pain, sorrow, grief and all the other hurts in life. He was here. He was one of us. He was a participant, not a mere spectator.

Consider the "man of sorrows" described in Isaiah 53:3-8. This prophecy described in detail centuries before His birth how Jesus would suffer and die. Read carefully, noticing especially the verbs. They are powerful words that describe intense suffering.

When we hurt, we must remember that God, the Creator of the universe, understands. Jesus, His Son, has experienced feelings and emotions just as we have. When we pray, we do not pray through some distant and unknowing being. Rather, we pray through One who has been there. We pray through one who has experienced the full range of human existence, including pain and even death.

Nothing in This Life Is Permanent

As human beings our understanding of life is very limited. Everything we know pertains to this physical existence. We know little about the spiritual world and even less about eternity. As Christians we must realize that nothing in this life is permanent. We were not created to remain here; we were created for another existence.

In the book *The Innocence of Father Brown*, the English essayist and poet G.K. Chesterton wrote about being on "the wrong side of the tapestry." On one side of a tapestry, one sees a beautiful picture woven of colored threads. But on the other side – the "wrong side" – one sees only knotted and uneven threads. The image is difficult or even impossible to see from the wrong side. As humans we can now see only one side of the tapestry, and it is the "wrong side." Our view of life and our understanding of the world are incomplete.

That's why the faith we have in God is so crucial. It provides the only means of making sense out of life and having any hope for the future. Only through faith can we see the whole picture, even from this "wrong side of the tapestry."

Faith Builders

1. How does the problem of pain relate to the fact that we humans have the ability to make choices?

2. How might the laws of the universe be a cause of pain?

3. In what ways do we see that life is not fair?

4. How would you explain Romans 8:28 in your own words?

5. What does it mean to say that Jesus was a "participant"? How does this affect our understanding of pain?

Mountain Movers

Unfortunately, Christians must suffer pain and face disasters that seem unfair and unexplainable. Sept. 11, 2001, was one such tragedy.

- Where were you when you first heard about the tragedy of Sept. 11, 2001? Are you old enough to remember? Were you watching on live television when the airplane hit the second tower?
- How have your feelings changed about that day now that you are older?
- Why did God allow that tragic day to happen?
- What is the most traumatic experience you have encountered in your life? How did you handle it?
- What part did God play in your grief resolution?

Enduring the sufferings and tragedies in our lives are never easy. Christians are not exempt from suffering hardships. How can our faith in God help strengthen us during these difficult times?

Life can be difficult. God doesn't promise us a life without problems and suffering, but He does always promise to be with us. We need to rely on our faith in Him.

- After studying this chapter, how would you answer a friend who asked you, "If there is an all-powerful, loving and kind God, why does He allow pain and suffering in the world?"
- Why doesn't God relieve Christians of evil and wickedness in their lives?
- Why do bad things happen even to God's people?

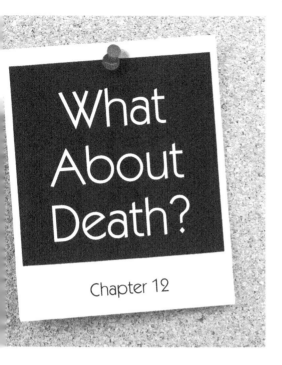

What About Death?

Chapter 12

"For if we have been united together in the likeness of His death, certainly we also shall be in the likeness of His resurrection" (Romans 6:5).

Mustard Seed Moment

If I hold up a glove in the air, I can tell that it has no life. It cannot move by itself. However, if I put the glove on my hand and move my fingers around, the glove comes to life, doesn't it? Think of the glove as a person's physical body. Think of my hand as his spirit. When the spirit enters the body, the body can move around and do things.

When we die, our body and spirit will be separated. When the spirit leaves the body at death, the body cannot move. After I take my hand out of the glove, the glove does not move. The body has died just as the empty glove has stopped moving. But the spirit is alive, just as my hand can still move around.

What do I do with a mustard seed? In this chapter, we will learn what the Bible says about death and the victory we can have in death. We need to remember that for a Christian, death is not the end. God's promise is that our spirits will live with Him forever if we have been faithful.

No Way to Escape It

Thousands of soldiers die in a single battle. A hurricane or an earthquake kills hundreds or even thousands of people. A jumbo jet crashes with no survivors. Death on such a scale is appalling and difficult to understand. Yet all of us will face death on a much more personal level –

in the death of a loved one or close friend, or in our own death.

Mankind has truly subdued the earth. We have conquered both land and sea and traveled to the moon. We have eliminated many diseases and prolonged the lives of many people. We have not, however, been able to conquer death.

Death has always been viewed as the enemy. The alchemists sought to prolong life with magic elixirs. Great explorers sought the "fountain of youth." Even today some people seek to extend life with special diets or exotic treatments. Death, however, is an inevitable part of living.

Death Is the Enemy

For many people death is the ultimate disaster. It is viewed as annihilation, extinction or the end of existence. It is the termination of life. We speak, for example, of a "terminal illness," which conveys the idea of the end of something. To some people, death is merely viewed as the end of physical life, but to others it is the obliteration of existence. Must we view death as the ultimate disaster? Is death really the termination or extinction of existence?

Those who are in Christ need not worry. Death is not the end; it is merely the beginning of something new. The fear, hopelessness and helplessness often associated with death are unnecessary. The empty tomb and resurrected Lord give us hope, even in death (Romans 6:5-10).

Death as a Symbol

How ironic that death is the symbol of entrance into the kingdom of God! Baptism is a symbolic death and the act that enables God to add the new Christian to the church, His kingdom (Acts 2:47). In baptism we are united with Christ (or share) in His death (Romans 6:3-5). Baptism is symbolic of the death of the body of sin and the resurrection of a new person. A person enters the water as the "old man of sin," symbolically dies, and rises from the water as a new creature (Romans 6:6-7).

Death for the Christian Is Not Final

Jesus said, "I am the resurrection and the life" (John 11:25). To us, however, our resurrection may seem far away. But we are not left without testimony regarding this resurrection. First, we have accounts in the New Testament of several people raised from the dead:

1. Jesus raised Jairus' daughter (Matthew 9:18-26), the widow's son at Nain (Luke 7:11-17) and Lazarus (John 11:1-44).
2. Peter raised Tabitha, or Dorcas (Acts 9:32-43).
3. Paul raised Eutychus (Acts 20:7-12).

The people in these examples were raised from the dead, but they returned to their previous existence. They lived a period of time and then died again. Their experience is not the same as that of the resurrection we are promised, but it does provide us insights into God's power over death.

The resurrection of Jesus is the greatest testimony of all. The others who had been raised from the dead went on to die again. Jesus, however, not only died and was raised again, but He also conquered death. He was raised from the dead never to die again (Romans 6:9-10).

I especially enjoy how J.B. Phillips, an English writer and Bible translator, has translated Romans 6:10: "We can be sure that the risen Christ never dies again – death's power to touch Him is finished." Death is the enemy, but the enemy has been defeated. When we are raised, as Jesus was raised, death will no longer have the power to touch us either.

The empty tomb and the resurrected Lord are the basis for our hope and assurance that death is not final. We need not fear death as the termination of existence. As Christians we cannot be touched by the power of death, for we share not only in the death of Christ but also in His resurrection (Romans 6:1-14; 1 Corinthians 15:20-28).

The Analogy of the Seed

As already noted, many people view death as the end or termination of life. For Christians, however, such is not the case, for the Bible teaches that death is simply the means of passing from one existence to another. Although we as Christians may have moments of worry, fear and even doubt, we need not be alone in those moments because death is a frequent topic in the Bible.

In one example, Paul uses an analogy of a seed to teach about death (1 Corinthians 15:35-44). Inside every seed is an embryo, or baby plant. The embryo is, in a sense, confined within the seed. The embryo's only means of escape is for the seed to be planted and allowed to germinate. In the soil, the seed splits open, the embryo is released from its prison, and a new life begins.

Such is our human existence. A part of us, our spirit, is immortal, but like the embryo in the seed, our spirit is housed in our physical body. In death, the spirit, like the embryo of the seed, is released from its imprisonment. Death, then, is an escape of our spirit from the confines of the physical body. Just as a seed germinates into a new plant, so shall we rise to a new existence in our spiritual body.

The Metaphor of Sleep

The New Testament writers also used the metaphor of sleep to describe death. Jesus used it to describe Jairus' daughter (Matthew 9:24) and also Lazarus (John 11:11). Perhaps the most striking usage of this metaphor was in the description of the death of Stephen, who was stoned by an angry mob (Acts 7:60).

Since the earliest days of the church, the metaphor of sleep has described death – a comparison that contrasted with the view of death found in Greek and Roman thought of the day. Hopelessness and finality were replaced with the metaphor of sleep and subsequent awakening. In the commentary *Word Studies in the New Testament*, minister and author M.R. Vincent explains how Christianity altered the view of death: "The pagan burying-place carried in its name no suggestion of hope or comfort. It was a burying-place, a monumentum, a mere memorial of something gone ... but the Christian thought of death as sleep, brought with it into Christian speech the kindred thought of a chamber of rest, and embodied it in the word 'cemetery' – the place to lie down to sleep" (83).

The Christian and Hope

The word "hope" is used in everyday language typically to express a wish or desire. When used in the Bible, however, the word "hope" carries with it an expectation or anticipation. As Christians, our hope is based first in the death and resurrection of Jesus (Romans 6:5-10; 1 Corinthians 15:54-57) and in the promises God has made (Romans 8:18-28).

When we look at the world, we begin to wonder about this hope. All around us we see a world of sin, crime, pain, disease and death. After all, everything we understand about this life points to death, destruction and decay. How can anyone believe in the resurrection? Even a Christian, in anger and frustration, may be tempted to ask, "What hope?"

The complete answer, however, will never come in this life. Only in the next life can we ever have an answer to such pressing questions. It is unreasonable not to believe in the resurrection. The alternative is too stark, too bleak and too meaningless. If life is nothing more than a short period of physical existence, then it is hardly worth the bother. Only the hope of the resurrection can give any meaning to life and peace in death.

I do not know what it is like to die, to be resurrected, or to live in eternity. I just know that it will be better. There will be no pain, unhappiness, sorrow or death. There will be no loneliness or sadness. No disease of any kind will be there. All these woes of the world will be left behind as we move from this life to the next (Revelation 21:1-4).

Death is the enemy, but the enemy has been vanquished. This is the good news that was preached by the earliest disciples of Jesus and the hope that we too have in Christ.

Faith Builders

1. How do people today commonly view death?

2. What assurances do we have that death is not final?

3. Why do even Christians at times worry about dying?

4. What is the significance of "sleep" as a metaphor for "death"?

5. Where is the hope that we have as Christians?

Mountain Movers

People have many questions about heaven.
- Will we know each other in heaven?
- Are all good people going to heaven? What does the Bible say? How would you explain your answer to another person who does not believe as you do?

- In Jesus' teaching of the rich man and Lazarus, what do we learn about what happens when we die (Luke 16:19-31)?
- What does the Bible teach us about judgment day? Read John 5:28-29; Revelation 20:13-15.
- If we are promised "no tears in heaven," what about our loved ones who aren't there (Revelation 21:4)?

Sometimes there are no concrete answers to our questions. We will have to find out when we get to heaven. We have to have faith that somehow God will fulfill His promise that heaven will be greater than anything we could ever imagine.

- How important are the verses in Revelation 22:18-19 to the world, even the religious world today?
- How does the lesson of our faith as a mustard seed – so tiny at first but growing into a large tree – apply to our purpose in life while we are here on earth?

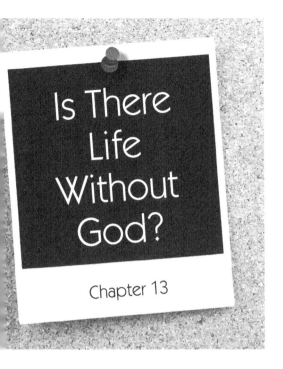

Is There Life Without God?

Chapter 13

"Then [Jesus] said, 'What is the kingdom of God like? And to what shall I compare it? It is like a mustard seed, which a man took and put in his garden; and it grew and became a large tree, and the birds of the air nested in its branches' " (Luke 13:18-19).

Mustard Seed Moment

The decision to become a Christian is a very serious and individual one. Those who are mature enough in their own thinking to understand the teachings of the Bible, repent of their sins, confess Jesus as God's Son, and demonstrate faith in Jesus are ready to be baptized.

A good definition of repentance is to picture a man walking toward the edge of a cliff. If the man keeps walking that direction, he will fall off the cliff – and probably plunge to his death below. Picture the man coming right to the edge of the cliff but then turning completely around and going back the other way. That is repentance. A person is doing the wrong thing but then decides to turn his or her life around to do the right thing and make better choices.

What do I do with a mustard seed? The Bible teaches that we are to confess that we believe that Jesus is the Son of God and then be immersed in baptism for the forgiveness of our sins. Jesus died on the cross so we could have that privilege! In this chapter, we will learn of biblical examples of baptism and the blessings of our lives with God. We certainly don't want to live our lives without God. He will supply all of our needs if we just have faith in Him. Even as our faith starts out tiny like a mustard seed, God will help it grow greater than we can imagine!

The Only Thing That Makes Life Livable

I really cannot understand what life without God would be like. I have known a few people who claimed to be agnostic or atheists. I have known far more, however, who simply lived their lives as if there was no God, whether they made any claim to that effect or not. History is filled with such people, and most of them lived lives of unhappiness and despair.

At its best, life can be difficult, but at its worst life can be almost unbearable. The only thing that can make life livable is God. Faith in God; faith in the Bible; faith in Jesus and His life, death and resurrection; and faith in God's promises – these are the things that make life worth living. In the end, they are the only things that truly matter.

Life with God begins with a new birth and a new life. We actually must die to our old way of living and begin new and fresh. The result is not only a new life but also blessings from God in this life and a place with Him in the next.

A New Life

The idea of a new start is something most of us find appealing. A new life is actually something God promises for each of us. Sometimes we call this being born again, or the new birth. We read about it in John 3:1-5, in which a ruler named Nicodemus came to Jesus, who explained how to have a new birth or a new life.

Jesus explained that in order to have a new life, one must first enter the kingdom of God – a simple task, but as Jesus pointed out, conditions must be met in order to do so.

Jesus told Nicodemus that a person must be born of the water and the Spirit. The water Jesus spoke about was baptism. After Jesus returned to heaven and the new kingdom was initiated on the Day of Pentecost (Acts 2), this teaching about baptism became more apparent. Peter, as we read in Acts, was the first to teach about the necessity of repentance and baptism (or the new birth) for entrance into God's new kingdom (2:38).

Jesus also told Nicodemus that one must be born of the Spirit. Baptism is an outer action – a person is physically immersed in water. Being born of the Spirit, however, is an inner action. It involves an inward change, known as repentance, and represents a complete reversal in the way the person thinks and lives.

Numerous examples of people experiencing this new birth are found in the book of Acts:

1. the believers on Pentecost (Acts 2:36-41);
2. the people of Samaria (Acts 8:9-25);
3. the Ethiopian eunuch (Acts 8:26-40);
4. Saul (Acts 9:17-19);
5. Cornelius and his family (Acts 10);
6. Lydia and her family (Acts 16:11-15);
7. the Philippian jailer (Acts 16:25-34); and
8. Crispus and others in Corinth (Acts 18:7-8).

In each of these cases, the individuals first believed, or had faith, in Jesus as God's Son; they repented, or desired to change their lives; and then they were baptized to enter the kingdom of God. In doing so they gained the new life that Jesus told Nicodemus about.

Baptism is the symbol of the new birth and the new life that comes through this birth. What exactly does baptism symbolize? Paul writes in Romans 6:1-10 that baptism first symbolizes the death, burial and resurrection of Jesus, along with the death of our old life and the resurrection to a new life.

What is the purpose of baptism? Its first purpose is to make possible our salvation and forgiveness of sins (Mark 16:15-16; Acts 2:38). Second, baptism puts a person into the body of Christ; the Lord adds him or her to the church (Acts 2:47; Galatians 3:26-27). Third, baptism allows Christians to receive spiritual blessings (Ephesians 1:3).

God Will Supply Our Needs

Additional blessings come from a new life in Christ and a new relationship with God. As a new Christian begins to live a life of faith, he or she discovers these blessings in everyday living. All of us have certain basic emotional or psychological needs, for instance. Living a life of faith supplies these needs in a person's life in a way that cannot be found elsewhere.

Everyone feels the need for acceptance. This is the most basic of human needs, yet so many people in our world lack a sense of belonging. When we look at the life of Jesus, we see that He accepted others regardless of their status in life. He even took time to be with the social outcasts of His day, including a Samaritan woman (John 4:1-29), a blind beggar named Bartimaeus (Luke 18:35-43), and the tax collector Zacchaeus (Luke 19:1-10).

Jesus expressed concern for all people. He also died for all people – with no exceptions. Although some people do not recognize or appreciate this fact, Jesus still died for them.

In God's kingdom we are all the same (Galatians 3:26-29). Our status does not depend on any human qualifications. We are one in Christ.

Along with a need for acceptance, all people need to feel secure, and Christians have the greatest security of all: heaven (John 14:1-3). Heaven gives Christians something to live and die for. An atheist has nothing to live for and nothing to gain from dying, but a Christian has everything to live for and everything to die for.

We all need to feel loved. The word used for God's love is from the Greek word "*agape*," which is sometimes translated as "unmerited love." Agape is to love someone even when you're not loved in return. Some people are easy to love whereas other people are not. Agape love makes no distinction. God loves even the most unlovable.

Finally, each person feels the need to be responsible. A person needs something to live for, some purpose in life, and something to be responsible for. As Christians we have been given the responsibilities to live right in God's sight (Matthew 6:33), help others in need (25:41-46), and share God's message with others (28:18-20).

The Blessings of Being in Christ

In the New Testament the phrase "in Christ" indicates that a person is in the kingdom or in the church. God has promised various blessings to those who are "in Christ" (Ephesians 1:3). Each of these blessings is dependent upon being born again, being in Christ, and living a life of faith (Acts 2:37-38; Romans 6:1-4). These blessings include eternal life (6:23), freedom from condemnation (8:1), the gift of grace (1 Corinthians 1:4; Ephesians 2:8-9; 2 Timothy 1:9), forgiveness (Ephesians 4:32) and many others.

Life With God

Living a life of faith leads to a special relationship with God. As a new Christian rises from the water of baptism, he or she is reconciled with God (Colossians 1:21-23). The sins that once separated that person from God have been washed away, and he or she has a new relationship with the Father.

This new relationship with God includes not only fellowship with God Himself but also with other Christians (1 John 1:5-7). Brothers and sisters in Christ can be a source of encouragement as the new Christian begins to live the life of faith.

Finally, as a Christian, each of us also has the promise from God that He will be with us no matter what happens (Romans 8:28). In good times or bad, God will always be there.

A life with God is a life of faith – faith in what He has told us and faith in what He has promised. It is the best life anyone can live and is filled with blessings in this life and hope for the next.

Faith Builders

1. What is the "new birth"? How is a person "born again"?

2. How did people in the first century become Christians or "born again"?

3. What is symbolized by baptism?

4. What are some of our needs that God will supply?

5. What does it mean to be "in Christ"?

Mountain Movers

We must have faith in God that He will provide for our needs in the good times and bad. In 1 Peter 5:6-9, Peter told his readers to resist the devil and be "steadfast in the faith, knowing that the same sufferings are experienced by your brotherhood in the world." Peter was writing to Christians who were suffering because of their faith in Jesus. Peter tells them that their present trials will prove that their faith is genuine.

- Why is it that when problems arise in our lives, we sometimes question our faith?
- Have you ever had to suffer for making the right decision?
- Have you ever been ridiculed for taking a stand against something that was wrong?
- Have you ever had to stand alone for what was right?
- Have you ever disagreed with other Christians in a decision of what was right or wrong? Share examples with the class.

As Christians, we have a special relationship with God. He provided a way, through the death of His Son, for us to have forgiveness of our sins. Even as Christians, we will not live perfect lives, but God perfects us by His grace and forgiveness if we remain faithful to Him.

Think about the experiences that led you to become a Christian.

- What people were most influential in your spiritual growth to reach that decision for your life?
- How did you know that you were ready to be baptized?
- Truthfully, has your faith and enthusiasm for being a Christian grown since the time you were baptized, or has it stagnated?
- If your faith has grown, in what ways?
- If your faith has stagnated, what can you do about that?
- If you haven't become a Christian yet, what questions or concerns do you have? Pray earnestly that you can make that decision soon. Study what you need to know to prepare yourself for this very important decision.

Remember, God has promised that if we have even the faith of a tiny mustard seed that our faith can grow so large that we can actually move the mountains in our lives. We just need to have the kind of faith that will allow Him to truly affect our lives and show us just what He can do!

So what do we do with our mustard seed of faith? Plant it, keep it nurtured, and watch God make it grow!

Chapter 5

Blanton, Dana. "More Believe in God Than Heaven." *Foxnews.com* 18 June 2004. <http://www.foxnews.com/story/ 0,2933,99945,00.html>.

Taylor, Humphrey. "While Most Americans Believe in God, Only 36% Attend a Religious Service Once a Month or More Often." *Harris Interactive.* The Harris Poll #59. 15 October 2003. <http://www.harrisinteractive.com/harris_poll/index.asp?PID=4 08>.

Chapter 6

Fillon, Mike. "Real Face of Jesus: December 2002 Cover Story." *Popular Mechanics* December 2002. *Popularmechanics.com.* <http://www.popularmechanics.com/science/research/1282186. html>.

Martin, Ralph P. "Jesus Christ." *International Standard Bible Encyclopedia.* Vol. 2. Grand Rapids: Eerdmans, 1982.

Chapter 7

Barclay, William. *The Gospel of John.* Vol. 1. Daily Study Bible Series. Philadelphia: Westminister John Knox Press, 1975.

Tenney, Merrill C. *John: The Gospel of Belief.* Grand Rapids, Mich.: Eerdmans, 1948.

Chapter 8

Simmons, Randy. *Basic Training.* Nashville, TN: Gospel Advocate, 2000.

Chapter 12

Vincent, M.R. *Word Studies in the New Testament.* Vol. 3. Grand Rapids, Mich.: Eerdmans, 1975.

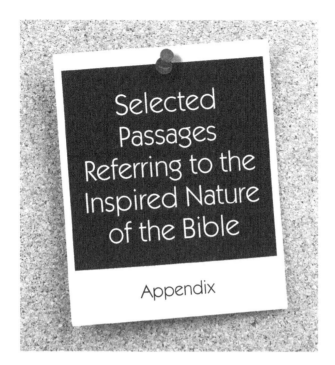

Selected Passages Referring to the Inspired Nature of the Bible

Appendix

Exodus 4:10-16; 31:18; 32:15-16; 34:1

Numbers 22:28-38; 23:12, 16, 23-26

1 Samuel 10:9-12

2 Samuel 12:7-9; 23:1-2

Psalms 19:7-11; 119:9, 89, 97-105

Isaiah 1:10-18; 30:8-15; 55:6-11

Jeremiah 1:4-9; 23:16-22, 28-31, 36; 26:2, 8; 36:4-8, 14-19, 20-25, 27-30

Ezekiel 3:4-11; 11:1, 5

Daniel 2:19-23, 26-28

Amos 3:1, 7-8; 7:12-16

Micah 3:8-12

Matthew 1:22; 2:4-6; 4:4, 7, 10; 5:18; 15:1-9; 22:29-32, 42-45

Luke 16:29-31; 24:25-27, 44-45

John 5:38-40, 45-47; 6:63; 7:16-17; 8:26, 28, 31-32, 40, 47; 10:35; 12:47-48; 16:13-14; 17:8, 17, 20

Acts 1:16; 4:25; 13:17-22, 29-30, 38-39; 20:32-35; 24:14

Romans 3:2; 9:17

1 Corinthians 2:13; 14:37

2 Corinthians 13:8

Galatians 1:8-12; 3:16

Ephesians 1:13

1 Thessalonians 2:13

1 Timothy 4: 1, 16

2 Timothy 2:15, 25; 3:7, 15-17; 4:2-4

Titus 1:9, 14

Hebrews 1:1, 6-8; 4:4; 5:12; 10:15

James 1:18-22

1 Peter 1:10-12

2 Peter 1:19-21; 3:15-16

1 John 4:6; 5:10-11

2 John 1-10

Jude 3

Revelation 2:7, 11, 17, 29; 3:6, 13, 22; 22:18-19

Suggested Readings

Barnett, Paul. *Is the New Testament Reliable?* Downers Grove, IL: InterVarsity Press, 2003.

Brand, Dr. Paul and Philip Yancey. *The Gift of Pain: Why We Hurt and What We Can Do About It.* Grand Rapids, MI: Zondervan, 1997.

Bruce, F.F. *The New Testament Documents: Are They Reliable?* Grand Rapids, MI: Wm. B. Eerdmans, 2003.

Evans, C. Stephen. *Why Believe? Reason and Mystery as Pointers to God.* Grand Rapids: Eerdmans, 1996.

Geisler, Norman L. and Frank Turek. *I Don't Have Enough Faith to Be an Atheist.* Wheaton, IL: Crossway Books, 2004.

Green, Michael. *Who Is This Jesus?* Vancouver, BC: Regent College Publishing, 2007.

Habermas, Gary R. *The Historical Jesus: Ancient Evidence for the Life of Christ.* Joplin, MO: College Press, 1996.

Habermas, Gary R. and Michael R. Licona. *The Case for the Resurrection of Jesus.* Grand Rapids: Kregel, 2004.

Kaiser, Walter C., Jr. *The Old Testament Documents: Are They Reliable and Relevant?* Downers Grove, IL: InterVarsity Press, 2001.

Lightfoot, Neil R. *How We Got the Bible.* Grand Rapids: Baker, 2003.

McGrath, Alister. *Doubting: Growing Through the Uncertainties of Faith.* Downers Grove, IL: InterVarsity Press, 2007.

Strobel, Lee. *The Case for Christ: A Journalist's Personal Investigation of the Evidence for Jesus.* Grand Rapids: Zondervan, 1998.

Strobel, Lee. *The Case for Faith: A Journalist Investigates the Toughest Objections to Christianity.* Grand Rapids: Zondervan, 2000.

Yancey, Philip. *Disappointment With God: Three Questions No One Asks Aloud.* Grand Rapids, MI: Zondervan, 1992.

Yancey, Philip. *The Jesus I Never Knew.* Grand Rapids: Zondervan, 2002.

Yancey, Philip. *Reaching for the Invisible God: What Can We Expect to Find?* Grand Rapids: Zondervan, 2002.

Yancey, Philip. *Where Is God When It Hurts?* Grand Rapids: Zondervan, 2002.

CPSIA information can be obtained at www.ICGtesting.com
Printed in the USA
BVOW10s1417301113

337776BV00008B/129/P